LET GO AND BE FREE: 100 DAILY REFLECTIONS FOR ADULT CHILDREN OF ALCOHOLICS

VOLUME 1

RON VITALE

Copyright © 2020 Ron Vitale

All rights reserved.

ISBN: 978-1-7368780-7-1

Visit Ron Vitale's website at www.RonVitale.com

Mom, thank you for teaching me to never give up and reach for the stars.

ALSO BY RON VITALE

- *Let Go and Be Free: 100 New Daily Reflections for Adult Children of Alcoholics (Volume 2)*
- *Let Go and Be Free: 100 More Daily Reflections for Adult Children of Alcoholics (Volume 3)*
- *Let Go and Be Free: 100 Final Daily Reflections for Adult Children of Alcoholics (Volume 3)*

INTRODUCTION

I grew up in an alcoholic and dysfunctional family and dealt with the shame of that for the past four decades. I've gone to therapy, Adult Children of Alcoholics Anonymous meetings, read self-help books, and did everything I could to find out how to overcome my upbringing. To help share what I've learned, I decided to write this book. If you struggle with having been raised in an alcoholic and dysfunctional family, then I'm here to help. You are not alone, and I want to shine a light on the challenges I struggle with so that you can help yourself. I invite you to come on a journey with me. You can read the daily meditations in order or randomly, it doesn't matter. What's important is that you choose to step out on a journey to discover how to heal.

DAY 1: WELCOME TO LET GO AND BE FREE

Today is day one of a new writing adventure that I'm starting. It's called "Let Go and Be Free." I wanted to share some thoughts about meditation, dealing with emotions, and how to be your best self.

To get started, here's a little bit about me. I grew up in a dysfunctional home. My father drank, smoked pot, and abused my mom. After my mom divorced my dad, she, my little brother, and I moved into my grandparents' home.

For the longest time, I used my imagination to help me deal with and escape all the problems in my life. As a kid growing up, I didn't know about dealing with all the emotions and feelings that I felt.

I remember my father having visitation rights and how angry I'd feel when he brought one of his girlfriends along with him on our day together. It's funny when I look back and the little things that I remember decades later. One Christmas I received a bike from my father and liked it. My father was supposed to bring over an ornamental number plate that you put on the front of the bike, but he either forgot or never made the effort. The hurt that I felt from that stayed with me for a long time. I felt cast off and abandoned.

But around the time I turned seven years old, my father was out of the picture.

Money was tight in our household, and I remember how angry I'd get in learning that my father never gave my mom any money for my brother and me. Back then you couldn't garner someone's wages to have him pay alimony, so he just went his way, and we did the best we could. I carried anger within that grew like a diamond in my heart, and for a long time, I harbored that pain as a shield that would protect me from the world.

I grew up, started dating, and realized that I kept falling into the same patterns. I didn't seem to be able to have a relationship that lasted longer than two years. I believed in true love and soulmates, but I'd meet someone, and things would fall eventually fall apart.

The worst side of me would come out: I expected everyone to push themselves as hard as I worked, and I would judge my partner's actions like there was no tomorrow.

When people talk about how alcoholism directly affects the next generation, I didn't quite understand that, but now I do. Though I'm not an alcoholic, I have struggled with the behaviors associated with living in an alcoholic and dysfunctional family.

Only recently did I learn of the Adverse Childhood Experiences (ACE) study that scores the different types of abuse and neglect you've encountered as a child and makes an estimate on how you are likely to have a higher risk of health problems in life.

I didn't know that the test even existed. But over the years of broken relationships, feeling shame and lost, I stumbled upon Adult Children of Alcoholics Anonymous (ACOA) and found some healing there. I also spent time going to counselors and therapists over the years so that I could find a way to become a better person and to heal.

As I grew older, I wanted to have my own family, and I didn't want to repeat what I went through as a child As a young adult, I felt broken and damaged. Often, I felt so alone because I couldn't find anyone who could identify with what I had gone through.

Healing Comes from Within

I'm starting this "let go and be free" adventure because I want to share what I've learned along the way. Even if only one person reads what I write and finds something helpful, then my work will have been worth the effort.

If you've read this far and can identify with what I've written, then here's where the journey begins. It's a new day. A brand-new day starts today with limitless possibilities.

The topics that I'll discuss will be like these:

- I'll share helpful books that I've read

- podcasts that I listen to that help ground me
- amazing movies that I've seen
- and I'll share my successes, my failures and
- even my clumsy experiments in learning yoga after I pulled out my back from running.

I expect that over time, the blog will evolve and grow. We shall see together.

I hope you come along with me on the journey.

Thank you.

DAY 2: HOW TO DEAL WITH THE STRESS AND ANXIETY FROM RUMINATIVE THOUGHTS

When I was 23 years old, my fiancée broke up with me for good. I sat at my desk and struggled to finish my graduate schoolwork while the diamond engagement ring sat in a drawer right next to my desk. My anxiety level had gone through the roof. I had a challenging time focusing on my work because I kept having a tape play in my head: "She's broken up with you. She doesn't love you anymore. You suck. It's all over for you."

The thoughts kept circling in my head, and I could not find a way to stop ruminating on the problem. No matter how hard I tried, my brain kept bringing me back to the breakup and I felt horrible about how things had fallen apart.

What I have learned from that time is that there is a way to help break the cycle of anxiety and stress. It's not easy to do, but I want to share with you what has worked for me over the years in dealing with ruminative thoughts. I do hope that these techniques will be useful to you.

Progressive Muscle Relaxation

Close your eyes and take a deep breath while slowly clenching your left fist. Keep your left fist clenched tight for a few seconds and then as you exhale (slowly), release your fist. Take four seconds or so breathing in, hold three seconds, then exhale slowly out of your mouth while unclenching your fist. When finished, do it again.

Repeat the process with your right fist, left foot and then right foot (by bending in your toes as you inhale), clench your teeth, squeeze tight your eyes, shrug and hold your shoulders, do the same for your pelvic floor muscle (like doing Kegel exercises), and then lastly tighten all your muscles at once, breathing in slowly through your nose, hold a second or two, and then exhale from your mouth slowly.

I found the above exercise to be not only a fantastic stress reliever but also a way to recharge my batteries. It's an excellent way to soothe me and relax.

Light Visualization Exercise

If I have a few more minutes, I perform the following visualization technique. I lie on my back, relax, and slowly breathe in through my nose. While breathing in, I imagine a warm light entering me, permeating its way through my cells, in my blood, and through my nerves, muscles, and bones. The light cleanses as it passes through me. After a few seconds, I then exhale all the darkness, hate, and stress within me. I imagine impurities streaming out of my mouth as I exhale.

I then imagine the light traveling down through my body per breath. I breathe in a few seconds, and the light goes all through my head, out my mouth, ears, and eyes, then down my throat, and through my shoulders, and I hold it there. On exhaling, all the fear and darkness within me is slowly expunged from my body. When I take my next breath, the light continues past my shoulders, around and through my heart, and into my lungs, filling me with goodness and light. I continue doing this until the light has completed its journey all through my body and down through my toes.

Dealing with Incessant Anxiety

Before I knew about the two techniques above, I struggled with anxiety and had no idea what to do. What helped me back when I was in my 20s was a repetitive phrase that helped me deal with my ruminative thoughts. I'd do the following: I'd allow myself to think all the horrible things that ran through my brain but would cut things off after about 2 minutes. I'd then repeat over and over again a phrase that would be positive and help me break the cycle of ruminative thoughts.

Phrases that have worked for me:

- Let go, let God.
- I know I can, I know I can, I know I can.
- Yes. Yes. Yes. Yes.

When I first had to deal with the ruminative thoughts after the breakup back when I was in graduate school, the cycle would go like this: I'd deal with the pain and ruminative thoughts as best I could, go to sleep, wake up and be okay for a few minutes, but then a smell, a memory or some other reminder of the breakup would put me right back into feeling bad again.

I'd then use the phrases as a mantra to break the cycle. When the anxiety would get too bad, I even tried carrying a serenity prayer coin in my pocket. The prayer ("God grant me the serenity to accept the things I cannot change, the courage to change the things I can and wisdom to know the difference") was engraved on one side and "Let go, let God" was on the other. I'd rub my thumb over the words as I said the prayer repeatedly.

If you don't believe in God, change the phrases ("Let go, let be" and "Serenity to accept the things…") by removing the word God.

I've used these techniques for decades, and when I incorporate them all together, I have a much more robust set of skills to help me deal with ruminative thoughts, stress, and anxiety.

I hope these techniques are helpful to you.

And one last bit of wisdom: If you're ashamed of having to deal with anxiety and ruminating thoughts, I hope my story helps you see that you're not alone.

DAY 3: GRATITUDE

Today we celebrate Thanksgiving in the United States. It's never been one of my favorite holidays. In growing up, Thanksgiving meant dealing with my mom's second husband's relatives and pretending to like them. Or, as I got older, having distant relatives try projecting their prejudices on me.

One of my favorites is a relative on my wife's side of the family, who once told me: "Your people get very emotional." What a "wonderful way" to describe someone who is Italian. Oh well, those times have passed, and now Thanksgiving is a bit different.

Much of my family has either passed on or moved away.

The same is true for my wife's relatives.

Thankfully, everyone has been okay in combining the celebration of the holiday at our house. It's the best of both worlds in that we get to celebrate and be thankful for our whole family and not just one "side."

But this year, I have a lot of heavy thoughts on my mind. I'm dealing with lots of stress and have been using this "Let Go and Be Free" writing experience as a means to help myself and to share what I'm learning with others.

Thanksgiving is a time of gratitude and sharing with family and friends.

Earlier this week, some of my coworkers and I volunteered to feed the homeless at a local community center. I arrived and helped hang up donated clothes, and was told that on the day before Thanksgiving, the center would be opened and people could take the clothes that they need. There were old shoes, dress shirts, pants, sweaters along with children's hats and gloves for the approaching cold weather.

When the community center opened up to serve breakfast, my job was to great people as they came in. We took in five people at a time, and I'd smile, look them in the eye and say, "Good morning. Welcome."

Some people would smile back and wish me a good morning. A few appeared to be on drugs and high as they shuffled in to get a warm plate of food.

The center served eggs, potatoes, oatmeal, and a cup of coffee.

I don't have an exact count, but I believe we served around 150 people that morning.

On the way out, I asked people if they wanted a peanut butter and jelly sandwich. They were in plastic Ziplock bags in two large tubs. The PB&Js were several days old, and some had already started to get hard, but it was all we had.

I'm honored that I could volunteer and help people in the community, but I will be honest in that the need is so much greater than what we had to give out. Breakfast was served from 9 a.m. to 11 a.m., and the doors were promptly shut then as the food had all been given out.

I'm a people watcher, so I was able to see and listen to all sorts of conversations. I think the most surprising thing was seeing other people's reactions to my holding a roll of paper towels. Coffee spills happened often, and I'd get down to wipe the spill up so that no one slipped. But as soon as I ripped off a sheet from the roll, people would come up to me and ask, "Can I have a sheet?" They'd point to the paper towel roll, and I'd give them a sheet.

After a bit of this, one of the regular volunteers came up to me and told me that we had to hide the paper towels. If we didn't, we'd give them all out and wouldn't have anything left for the center to clean up spills.

Something that's so insignificant in my life, a few sheets of paper towel, was a luxury for the people we served.

Before my service time ended, a volunteer told us this story:

"One time we were about to close up and a man came in hungry. We had no food left, so I prayed to God and asked him to give me a miracle because there was nothing left to eat. As the man came toward me, I was about to turn him away when four people who were eating, took their plates of food and gave a quarter of their portion to the hungry man. It was a miracle."

I'm grateful this Thanksgiving that I could serve and help others. I know that it was only for a few hours and it won't change the massive problems we have in my country, but the fact remains is that we helped people that day. Not only with some food, but a warm smile, some pleasant conversation and we looked people in the eye and really saw them.

As I celebrate with my family and am thankful for the food on my table that I can share with those I love, I wanted to take a moment to reflect on the bounty I have and to be humble in giving of my time (and money) to help others.

Happy Thanksgiving.

DAY 4: BEING VULNERABLE IS NOT A WEAKNESS

I grew up in a family in which the men often didn't share their feelings. Or when they did, they expressed anger. Because I didn't have many great male role models in my life, my best friends have always been women.

I identify more with women and think that this all goes back to being raised primarily by my mom and grandmother.

Mix in my creativity, being an introvert and my love of the arts and I'm a bit of a strange bird. I'm a misfit to most men and get poked fun at because I like the Indigo Girls, Tori Amos, and Sarah McLachlan.

I've never been shy to admit who I am and

what I believe, but I often keep quiet for fear that my worldwide doesn't mesh with what's popular.

I don't fit the typical male stereotype who loves watching football on Sunday and pounding down beers.

But where I really go off on my own, is my discussion of the power of vulnerability. I've mentioned shame researcher Brené Brown before and I'm a big admirer of her. I came across her wildly popular "The Power of Vulnerability" TED talk from back in 2010.

I grew up thinking that sharing my true self would be dangerous and laughed at because of how different I am.

My mom went through two divorces and suffered through verbal and physical abuse. At a young age, I learned that men can be powerful by inflicting their pain and suffering on those they supposedly love. And worse yet, I mirrored that behavior in my own relationships. I'm ashamed to admit that I have directed my anger at those I love. I've been verbally abusive and that's something that I'm deeply ashamed of.

You see, in growing up, I saw how the men in my life would take their feelings out on the women around them. And in living in an alcoholic/abusive family, I learned those behaviors and have worked hard through therapy, the Twelve Steps of Adult Children of Alcoholics Anonymous, and meditation to deal with my feelings.

Being vulnerable and opening up is hard because the world sees me "as a good guy." But I'm human.

The important thing that I've learned over the years is the necessity to work on myself. Not to "fix the broken parts" of me. No, that's not it at all.

But I have learned to embrace and accept who I am and how I grew up.

When I am stressed out and feel attacked, my instinct is to lash out in anger. I surround myself with words to project a strong offense.

Yet what I've taught myself over the years, is to think about the little kid in me who is freaking out and wants to lash out at people because I'm scared and feel threatened. As sappy as it might sound, mentally giving myself a hug and saying to myself that I'm here for myself helps settle me.

Yes, I'm a grown man approaching 50 years old who gives himself a hug when I feel down and threatened.

I'm choosing to be vulnerable because I believe that there are many, many other men out there who feel the way I do but can't admit to it. Society frowns on men showing weakness.

I can already hear the cynical throw their slings and arrows and making fun of me.

But here's the thing: I've carried such pain for decades. I've hidden my weaknesses from others because I was afraid.

Growing up in an alcoholic/dysfunctional family environment may not make you an alcoholic, but you damn sure are going to take up some of those traits:

- Hyper responsibility
- Lashing out in anger when you can't control your environment
- Trying to be prepared for any eventuality.
- Always thinking the worst will happen

The list goes on and on but naming the dysfunctional personality traits and shining a light on them does help. Do I still feel weak and shame? Yes, I do.

Here's the thing: Each of us has a choice. We can keep pretending and see where that gets us. Or we can take a chance and be brave. Be vulnerable.

I credit Brené Brown for helping me come to realize that I'd rather try than to keep hiding. Burying my feelings and pretending all is okay doesn't solve anything.

I choose to take a risk and to show my warts to the world to help heal myself, but also to share with other men out there—you're not alone.

Try being vulnerable. It might just lead you down a joyful path that you never could have imagined.

DAY 5: THE RESTORATIVE POWER OF SLEEP

When I was younger, I would stay up until the sun rose playing the card game *Magic: The Gathering*. I attended graduate school at night from 6:30 p.m. until 9:30 p.m. and then I'd go out with my friends.

I didn't focus on the importance of sleep.

I'd go home and get 4 or 5 hours of rest and then go about doing my schoolwork and going to my job. I had a lot of work on my plate.

But I didn't understand the importance of sleep.

Now that's different. I have prioritized sleep in my life. Just as I focus on the importance of exercise, eating healthy and practicing meditation.

How simple it is to focus on the restorative power of sleep, but for many years I did not make sleep a priority in my life.

I pushed and pushed myself to work harder and to get as much done as I possibly could each day. Without sleep, I can't dream. Without sleep, I'm not able to have my unconscious mind be free to be creative and help me write the stories that I turn into books.

When my son was born, my wife and I did not sleep much during those first two years of my son's life. He had many earaches as a baby and was up a lot. My wife and I tried to get as much sleep as we could, but those first two years were tough.

I still remember the first night when my son came home from the hospital after being born. He kept waking up crying every 45 minutes. As new parents, my wife and I had no idea what to do. He was breastfed, changed, held and loved, but he still kept crying nearly every hour. Over time he grew and after two years he began sleeping through the night.

Over the years, the lack of sleep affected me.

When I don't get enough sleep, I have a difficult time concentrating and making decisions.

Time has passed and I'm in a different stage of my life, but still have problems with sleep.

I follow strict rules regarding sleep:

- I keep no phone by my bed.
- I drink no caffeine after 5 p.m.
- I make time to unwind before bed by reading a few pages of a book.
- When I can't sleep, I'll use visualization and anxiety-freeing meditations to help me.
- I take naps on the weekends when I can.
- If I could go back in time, I would tell my younger self to get more rest. Sleep helps both my body and mind.

But since I can't time travel, I take getting my sleep seriously now. I need my rest and have created a boundary around that time. Sleep is key to my health and I make certain I treat it as such.

DAY 6: HOW TO DEAL WITH IRRATIONAL FEAR

I grew up in a dysfunctional household and what I experienced as a kid is now part of my DNA as an adult. If you grew up in a similar environment (alcohol, drugs, abuse, divorce, dysfunction, etc.), does this experience ring a bell with you?

Recently, my wife and I were arguing about finances. We were talking numbers and I expressed my fear of not having enough money to pay the bills. We were looking at the number and things get tense.

In my head, I reverted right back to my 5-year-old self and felt extremely small and powerless. A huge wave of irrational fear came over me, and my brain started going a mile a minute. One second

I'm talking with my wife about the bills and the next I'm afraid that we'll not be able to make ends meet. From there, my brain took a giant leap, and I imagined that we were out on the street.

There are certain triggers that set me off.

Lack of money is one of those triggers.

As a boy, my mom went on welfare for a bit, I had to wear second-hand sneakers to school (which my classmates picked on me relentlessly) and when things became tight financially, my mom came to me and told me that she had to take my savings from my bank account to pay for bills.

Even writing those things sends a shiver down my spine.

I am instantly transported back to my grandparents' house. It was summer out, warm, near twilight, and my mom came to me to talk to me about the money I had saved over the last few years. All my birthday present money and allowance I have saved up my mom needed to help pay the bills. All the times that I took my bank book to the bank and deposited money came flashing back. In the '80s, you would give the bank teller your deposit slip, bank book, and they would take your money, put it in your account and then print out your latest statement directly in your bank book.

I used to look at that little book and be so happy that I had worked so hard to save the two hundred and so dollars that I had saved up.

When my mom said she needed the money, I wanted to give it to her, but I also worried that more would be taken from me. (And to be honest, part of me resented that she needed the money.) What if it wasn't enough? What were we going to do?

Coming back to the more recent present, when my wife and I talked about money, those old fears rose within me and stirred up deep-seated worries within me. As a kid, I worried about a lot (where I'd be going to school and if we had enough money for things along with where I would live).

The reality is that we weren't destitute.

My grandfather helped my mom out and took us into his home. We were never going to be kicked out on the street, and I did fine with having toys, clothes, and such. But as a kid, I didn't see things that way.

I internalized my fear.

The Fears of Our Childhood Can Control Us

But now decades have gone by, and I'm still triggered by the same fears that overwhelmed me as a kid. I have carried those scars with me for a long time. My mom went through two divorces. I went to four schools and moved three times from kindergarten to 8th grade. I lived with my mom and father, then my mom, brother, and I moved in with my grandparents, and then we moved out with my stepdad (and then back with my grandparents).

I had a lot of instability in my life, and those fears played out in my relationships.

Disagreements and arguments over money and other triggers would send me right back to when I was a kid. And it sucked.

For a long time, I didn't know why this was happening to me. I hadn't had the education, training, or help to set me on a better path.

But with counseling and therapy, along with practicing the Twelve Step program of Adult Children of Alcoholics & Dysfunctional families, I became more grounded.

I stopped being rudderless when a problem hit me.

Ways to Let Go of Fear

To overcome my fears, I use the following tools:

- Talk to someone about it. (Just admitting that I'm in the middle of deep fear from my childhood helps. Yes, I sometimes feel shame about that, but I've learned to deal with that and let it go.)
- I meditate (more on this in a bit).
- I run through the Twelve Steps in my head or say the Serenity prayer.

I think the hardest thing is first to admit that I have a problem.

When going through the laundry list of adult children of alcoholics, this particular trait hits me hard:

"We are dependent personalities who are terrified of abandonment and will do anything to hold on to a relationship in order not to experience painful abandonment feelings, which we received from living with sick people who were never there emotionally for us."

Who would ever want to admit to this? Seriously.

Wouldn't it be easier to hide this under a rock in the deepest part of the sea so that no one would ever, ever know how I truly feel?

Back when I was young, I did hide away my fear of abandonment, but then I kept repeating the same pattern in my relationships over and over and over again. Things got to the point that even I could see my faults.

Admitting a truth is hard, but also not impossible. To overcome the fear of my childhood and the struggles I have in my adult life, I have chosen to share what I'm going through. It helps me, helps my relationships, and allows me to see a path to solve a problem.

Which then leads me to therapy, Adult Children of Alcoholics Anonymous meetings, and meditation.

There is no "one size fits all" solution for overcoming the fear (for me of abandonment) that's triggered from one's upbringing. I've used a wide range of tools to help me over the years.

And most recently, I came across a meditation

by Deepak Chopra on Empowerment. I'm going through Chopra's 21-day Empowerment meditations, and I'm on day 7. During the meditation, Chopra says in his calming voice: "Your sense of security cannot be shaken."

He goes on to explain how we can free ourselves from fear by realizing that we can overcome fear and insecurity. Once we let go and just be, we realize that there are no strings holding us back.

Now maybe meditation doesn't work for you. Maybe you believe in God and put your faith in organized religion. Or maybe you believe there is a higher power that you trust will not let you fall. I can't say what will work for you, but I do know that when I do let go of a situation that I feel better as though a burden has been lifted from me.

So, to go back to the beginning: When I'm thinking about the bills and finances, I now have the means to stop and think through a situation. I can let go and put my trust in God, in a meditation practice, but more practically, I can listen to my adult voice and ask:

Is it true?

Is it true that my family will be homeless? Is it true that I need to let my past fears overcome me?

Is it true that my fear of abandonment is coming to fruition?

No, I don't have to allow that any longer. I'm in control of my future by **letting go of my past fears**.

When I first started going to therapy, my counselor at the time taught me about the three different voices within us:

- Our child voice ("I want the candy now!")
- Our parental voice ("You can't have candy until after dinner, and that's final!")
- And our adult voice ("Is it true that I need to have candy now?")

What I have worked on for my years is to develop my adult voice and to center myself so that I can let go of the fears that overwhelmed me as a child.

I hope these same tools will help you.

DAY 7: PRACTICING THE LOVING-KINDNESS MEDITATION

Last January, I promised myself that I would go to a meeting about recharging and dealing with burnout after work. When the night finally came, it was 4 degrees outside, and I didn't want to head out in the cold, but decided to go at the last minute.

And I'm so glad I did.

The instructor taught us the Loving-Kindness Meditation.

We closed our eyes and for about 2 minutes kept focusing on this mediation:

May I be happy

> May I be healthy
> May I be peaceful
> May I live with ease

Seems pretty easy, right?

I've been practicing the meditation before I get out of bed in the morning. I focus on the positive thoughts, and the instructor was right—over time, it has made a difference in my mood and how I go about my day.

After you get this part of the meditation down, you then move on to the next level. Instead of saying the words to yourself, you think of someone you don't like (or having problems with) and say the mantra them.

May they be happy
> May they be healthy
> May they be peaceful
> May they live with ease

What?
> You heard me right.

Now, this is a lot harder than I had ever thought.

Last Sunday, I went on my long run and thought of a person who had caused me some hurt lately. As soon as I thought the first line, my brain revolted and gave me a big fat, "NO!"

One minute I was running, and the next I was trying to convince myself to say the mantra for that person that I didn't get along with very well.

I had to wrestle with my thoughts as I thought of them.

In Christianity, Jesus taught to turn the other cheek to your enemy. I always found that to be hard to do because my first reaction is to go into defensive mode.

I need to keep working on the second level of the Loving-Kindness meditation. I keep failing at it because there's an emotional struggle within me. I'm trying really hard to get over my feelings and send good wishes to people that I don't get along with, but it's not easy. I'm being honest because I've found the first level of meditation to be like a healing salve on my tired body and mind. It's been a great help.

But the second level, well, I'll need more time for that.

And the third level is to think of the world:

May everyone be happy
> May everyone be healthy
> May everyone be peaceful
> May everyone live with ease

I find this one to be easier than the second level because it's a bit more distant. "Everyone" could be anyone. But if you think about it, this would mean that I wish that a criminal to be happy, healthy, peaceful, and live with ease. That doesn't sit well with me yet. I think I need more time to be enlightened because I still resist this one.

The funny thing is that our instructor told us that it took about 24 months for her to get out of level 1 to the next level. Now I understand why.

Letting go and sending positivity to others makes sense because it frees us from our hang-ups and our grudges. Is it easy? No!

If you're looking for a new meditation, I recommend giving Loving-Kindness a try.

DAY 8: MAKE YOUR DAILY INTENTION

When I wrote this, it's getting to the end of the year and the beginning of a new one. And so begins the TV commercials and morning shows that will start talking about your New Year's resolution.

Experts have shown that 80% of people fail to meet their resolutions.

That's a pretty depressing statistic.

Similarly, many people who go on diets eventually gain back the weight.

I decided a long time ago not to make New Year's resolutions or go on diets. Instead, I'm working on daily intentions to help me change my lifestyle.

Creating new and healthy habits is now so much easier. A lot is going on within our brain that we must overcome to create new neural pathways and change behavior.

If you're looking for a great book about habits, I highly recommend *The Power of Habit: Why We Do What We Do in Life and Business*.

I read the book a few years ago, and it changed the way I approach making a change in my life.

What I work on is creating simple changes each day that build over time.

Here's my weekly schedule.

(Okay, before I go too far. I know that the word "schedule" might freak some people out, but I hope you stick with me.)

- Monday: Meditate, write before work
- Tuesday: Run, meditate before work
- Wednesday: Meditate, write before work
- Thursday: Run, meditate before work
- Friday: Meditate, write before work
- Saturday: Write and then meditate
- Sunday: Run and then meditate

That's it.

I like to keep things simple and to go on autopilot so that I don't have to make lots of decisions early in the morning before work. The more energy I need to spend on deciding how/when to exercise, or what I'm going to meditate on, the less time I'll have for it.

I have my exercise and meditations all picked out in advance. My running clothes are put out the night before; the meditation is all set, so I only have to hit play on my phone to listen to the session.

By building a light (and flexible) schedule, I can set a daily intention. I start my day with positivity, and that helps me through my day.

If something comes up and I can't work in writing or meditation as planned, I'll do it later that day, or I can skip it. I try not to miss many days because meditation and running help me.

Over time I am slowly adding in other intentions: eating healthy, getting up from my desk at work and walking every hour, and drinking more water.

I'm looking to make life-long changes and

don't want to follow a fad diet or exercise craze. I want to do something that's going to work for the rest of my life. With that in mind, I believe that small building blocks of positive actions eventually create life-long habits that are sustainable and helpful.

If you're looking to start small, a simple experiment could be:

10 to 15-minute walk and short meditation or yoga (15-20 minutes).

If mobility is a challenge, there are lots of videos on YouTube for doing yoga in a chair.

I challenge you to think differently and find activities that will work for you. If 10-15 minutes is too long, make it 5. But whatever you decide, build the activity into your daily schedule and keep yourself accountable (with positive reinforcement for success, not punishment for missing a day).

What are your daily self-care routines?

DAY 9: MAKE YOUR OWN SUCCESS

"Nobody loves me." Or, "they're all out to get me." Or better yet: "I can't get a break."

Self-fulfilling prophecies are an easy way to build a defensive barrier around ourselves. By putting a negative thought out into the universe, we do so to protect ourselves from when the other shoe hits the ground.

Having grown up in an alcoholic/dysfunctional family, thinking of the worst (and preparing for it) allowed me always to be ready for whatever would be coming my way. But focusing on the negative shrouded the good things in my life.

What's the difference between waking up in the morning and saying:

"Today, I'm going to embrace what comes my way."

But compare that with:

"I'll be ready for when that one-two punch comes at me."

Being in a constant defensive posture limits our ability to grow and succeed.

How can we obtain our fullest potential if we don't allow ourselves to think openly?

What I am learning to do is to create possibilities for myself.

I've never believed that luck comes to people. I've been writing fiction now for decades, and I still struggle with translating that dream into a livable wage.

And yet the tendency is to look at the success of others and go: "How did they become an overnight success? They're making hundreds of thousands of dollars on their books—how did they do that so quickly?"

The reality is that the authors that make it to the limelight have put in their time and been working hard.

Instead of being jealous of someone else's success, why not congratulate them?

A therapist once told me to visualize what I

want to happen in my life. If you're going to give a big talk in front of a large audience, imagine yourself on the stage, doing great, and then completing the task.

I believe success comes to me because I allow it. What do I mean by that?

- Avoid self-sabotage (getting close to your goal and then failing because of deliberate mistakes you're making to slow your progress).
- Be open to what's possible.
- Actively be available and helpful: network, talk with people, share with them your goals, and listen to their ideas.

We make our luck because we sow the seeds of our success. Helping someone today might connect you with that colleagues' friend, who then connects you to their spouse, and that could lead to a new opportunity.

Consider this:

"Woe is me!"

Who is going to want to work with you? Heck, you're not even going to want to work with yourself.

"Good morning, nice to meet you!"

Being open and willing to succeed opens new doors and possibilities.

All of this might sound so simple and maybe even trite but think about the times in which you might have been held back from fear or worry.

And then think about the successes you've had in life: I know that I've succeeded when I tried something new, talked with people I had just met, and offered to help.

When I've volunteered to help create HTML pages back in 1999 at my job, over two years I positioned myself to get a promotion at my job. When I went to a poetry reading on my own, I met my wife.

I am not saying that you throw what you want out to the universe, like "The Secret," and then through magic, your wish becomes a reality. No, not at all.

What I am saying is that through hard work, you create a positive environment for your future self to be ready to accept success.

When you grow up in a dysfunctional family, it's challenging not to be caught in a cycle. To break free, it's essential to clear the mind and practice successful habits that will help you.

One small step today can lead you to climb that mountain of an obstacle down the road.

DAY 10: ALLOW YOURSELF THE TIME TO GRIEVE

I remember sitting on my girlfriend's floor and crying uncontrollably. My body shook, and when I tried to talk, I broke down again. We had had an intense talk, and somehow, my father had come up. At 21-years old, I hadn't seen him in about 15 years.

As I cried, the realization washed over me that I would never have certain experiences in my life:

- A dad throwing a ball to his son.
- His teaching me how to ride a bike.
- Giving me a high five for a good report card.

- Helping me through a rough time after being bullied at school.

It's funny on how easy it is to repress all those feelings, but eventually they work their way to the surface. A part of me just grieved at my loss and what I would never have.

Many years later, I had a similar experience. I stood in the room where my first child would be born, and I painted the ceiling. My wife had gone shopping, so I had time alone. On the radio, "Time to Say Goodbye" by Andrea Bocelli came on. My grandfather had just passed a few months earlier, and he loved that song.

I could have turned the radio off, but I let the song play, and I tried to sing to it. Again, I broke down and sobbed. I cried at missing my grandfather. In a matter of months, I lost both my grandparents.

The realization that neither of them would ever hold our child in their arms hurt.

I had wanted our kid to meet my grandparents. I wanted to be able to say to them: "Your Nan and Pop took us in when we had nowhere to go. I didn't have my father in my life, but my grandparents did the best they could. I promise you that I'll do everything I can to be there for you."

But wishes and dreams don't make a reality.

Just as I couldn't go back in time and rewrite my history so that I had a father in my life, I also couldn't bring my grandparents back. I needed to grieve the loss of my Nan and Pop right during the year that was supposed to be a year of joy. We had to attend funerals while my wife was pregnant and I just remember looking at her belly and wondering how this could all happen.

It was painful period and took time to heal.

I share these two examples because I see them differently. I needed to grieve in both circumstances, but the healing process was radically different for each case.

For my father, I needed to do two things:

- Let him go and self-parent myself. (I needed to become my own father and give myself the love that I never received from my father.)

- Meet with my father and resolve my issues with him (that did happen, by pure luck, several years before I was married).

I needed to grieve about the loss of my childhood, but then also see the possibility of what my future would bring. Self-love and self-healing would enable me to overcome the past. It took time, therapy, Adult Children of Alcoholic Anonymous meetings, reading, and lots of talks with those I love, but I've come to an understanding with my father.

I had the opportunity to ask him basic questions such as: "WHY?"

Why did you do X or Y? Why did you act that way?

His answers (and willingness to be honest with me) taught me a powerful lesson: He wasn't the demon that I had made him out to be. He had made mistakes and was human. It allowed me to forgive him over time.

With the loss of my grandparents, it took time

to heal the wounds. When our son came into the world, his smile acted as a powerful help to help us see the circle of life.

In trying to be the best husband and father that I could be, those roles helped me better understand what my father and grandfather were going through as I was a boy. My faults have come out as I'm human, and I now have a better understanding of the patience needed to be a good father.

Before I could ever be a good parent to my son (and then to my daughter), I needed to be good to myself first.

And the first step on that road is to grieve what I never had as a kid. Growing up in an alcoholic/dysfunctional family, I often felt like we lived on Mars compared to other families. But what I didn't understand as a kid is that no family is perfect. Every family has its problems.

What's important is admitting mistakes, making amends, and actively working to better the situation.

Which brings me back to grieving: It's okay to cry and feel sorrow. It's okay to feel.

I took those emotions and then loved my inner child because I realized that I deserved it.

That realization became the spark that inspired me on my journey. To become a good parent, I needed to be good to myself first. It seems pretty basic until you stop and try it.

DAY 11: UNBRIDLED JOY

When is the last time that you just laughed and laughed? When's the last time that you just let yourself feel such great joy that your whole body tickled with energy?

Take a moment to watch a baby laughing hysterically.

Babies find joy in the simplest of things. The world is new to them. They're open, curious, and willing to let their emotions wash over them.

As we grow older, we often put defensive barriers around ourselves. We protect by walling ourselves off from the world. But by protecting, we also numb or distance ourselves from those who care.

What if we decided to open our hearts today?

What if we chose to let our barriers down?

What if we gave ourselves the self-love we deserve?

But what if we threw caution to the wind and allowed ourselves to feel unbridled joy?

I wonder...

DAY 12: THE POWER OF STILLNESS AND RELAXATION

I am a type A person. A co-worker once joked, "You've cured cancer by the time I even get out of bed in the morning."

There's a flip side to that of course: I push myself hard and the stress does adversely affect me.

A few years back I set a schedule so that I'm either writing or exercising before work. Monday, Wednesday, Friday and Saturday are writing days while Tuesday, Thursday and Sundays are running days.

But I encountered a problem with all that: When you push yourself too hard, you eventually crack. Sure, I can go on like that for a while, but getting 5-6 hours of sleep a night and then being out of the house for work for 11 hours of the day doesn't leave me with much time to do all the other things I need to do in my life.

Instead of easing up, I sometimes cram too much in and then break down (either I get sick or I snap at the stupidest thing).

There's a better way and it might sound counter-intuitive.

Keep in mind that having grown up in a dysfunctional family that as the oldest child, I took on great responsibility. I often take on more than I can chew, and I'll get the work done, but I sacrifice my own health in the process.

Thankfully, I've gotten better at saying no and giving myself space to breath and relax.

Time and time again, when I'm overwhelmed, I've found that taking time to relax and being still is the best medicine.

When I can't find an answer to a problem, or I'm so stressed out that I don't know what is the best path to take, there is one simple thing that I can do that will help:

Unplug, sit still, close my eyes and focus on my breathing.

The Power of a Relaxed Mind

Go, go, go! That's my normal state of mind. I'm working, planning, strategizing and juggling a bunch of things all at the same time. The problem is that I've learned that multi-tasking really doesn't work. Striving to keep multiple balls up in the air at the same time might seem like a great idea in the short-term, but over the years, I've found that it's best to ease up, relax and give myself time to breathe.

The problem is that when stressed out we often want to push harder, go faster, do more.

That's usually the worst response for me.

Instead, taking time to unplug helps.

If the weather's nice, try the following:

- Go for a run (no headphones!)
- Take a walk (leave phone off)
- Sit in a quiet space and just relax

Now that we are so connected to the internet and have so many different influences on us each day

(TV, phone, computer, people, billboards, traffic, etc.) we often don't get time to just think.

That might be scary at first. When you give yourself time to think, all sorts of thoughts and feelings might rise to the surface. Hurt, fear, and worry could bubble up. But allowing ourselves time to feel and then accept those feelings is a way to cleanse them from our body and mind.

The light visualization exercise that I shared in Day 2 is a great activity to use to help intentionally clear the mind. I believe that our brains need to be rebooted from time to time. If we're not getting enough sleep, then taking time out of our day to **chill and be still** will help.

And the added benefit: When I'm relaxed, creative ideas always pop into my head. Every novel that I've written has come about because I've given myself the time to just think and relax.

I can push, push, and push harder OR I can take a step back, chill out a few minutes by unplugging and feel a lot better.

You would think that I would have this figured out by now, but don't feel bad if you struggle to let go. Be kind to yourself. In the long run, I've found that it works out best for me (and I feel a heck of a lot better) if I make time for stillness.

DAY 13: WHO ARE YOU?

Back in college, a professor asked us to define who we are. When it was my turn to speak, I said something like: "I'm a son, a brother, a boyfriend, a student, a grandchild, a writer, but underneath it all, I am me."

She liked my answer and was surprised at my ability to be so introspective at 18 years of age.

When I look at myself these days and ask, "Who am I?", there's a whole different aspect to that answer now that I am decades older.

My roles don't matter to me as much as they did when I was younger. So, I'm a worker, a writer, a husband, a father. All of those roles are great, but a lot of that is tied into how I define myself in the world.

For those of us who grew up in an alcoholic/dysfunctional family, the roles we played when young are tied into who we are today and some of our greatest weaknesses: Being over responsible, resistant to change, and fearful of abandonment.

To shine a light on one's feelings and to allow them to come to the surface is not easy. To grow, I believe it is necessary to come to terms with who we are and then to love those parts of ourselves.

It's funny, but in growing up, I tried my best to be the opposite of my father and to avoid the dysfunctional behaviors that I grew up in. But the harder I tried to cut those parts out of me, the more I struggled.

I couldn't understand it at first.

Why was this so hard? To NOT be like someone, doesn't it make sense to do the opposite?

Unfortunately, I learned the hard way that you cannot cut out a piece of yourself. To deny my inner self, was to deny who I was and what had influenced me to be who I am today.

Instead, I have focused on embracing and loving my imperfections.

It seems a bit odd at first, but when I peel the onion, even more, there's a deep realization that dawned on me: I am me.

I just am. For good or for ill, I'm not separate from the world. I am part of the world. Here's where things get a bit metaphysical but bear with me:

If everything around me is created on Earth and everything on Earth is part of the solar system and the solar system is part of the galaxy, then the galaxy is part of the universe, of creation. I am me. I am who I am. But I am a part of creation.

Okay, let's break that down a bit. If every single atom was created in the Big Bang, and I'm part of the evolution of that moment, then who I am is tied into the fabric of the universe. I've always liked the astronomer Carl Sagan as he coined the phrase: "We are star stuff."

If you've not seen that clip of Sagan from the PBS series Cosmos, be sure to check it out.

So, on the most cosmic scale, we are all beings of creation. The atoms that formed planets and asteroids and comets that seeded the Earth with organic materials eventually formed life. We are descendants from those primordial pools on prehistoric Earth. And now we have consciousness, can imagine, think, but most importantly, we have the power to love.

I ask that you take a moment today to think about who you are. What roles do you play, what roles can you grow beyond, and if you were to shed those roles, who exactly would you be?

Find that out and ask yourself: What would happen if I loved all of me? (The "good," the "bad," the "in-between.")

DAY 14: HOW TO TAKE CONTROL OF YOUR LIFE

I wish that I could say that there is an easy path for someone who grew up in an alcoholic/dysfunctional family. But I can say this: There are definite steps you can take to help yourself.

When I look back at my life, I see that there are some positive choices that I made that helped put me on a different path.

I decided to go to college and learn. Education is key to me. No matter my age, I believe in learning for life.

I also chose to go to counseling and to attend Adult Children of Alcoholics Anonymous (ACOA) meetings. And from there, I adopted living and working the Twelve Steps.

If you're not familiar with the Twelve Steps, they can be hard for some as they mention "God." What I've seen and read over the years, is that if you don't believe in God, then substitute the "God" for a higher power.

(I've heard people say that the process of letting go of something beyond them is extremely helpful. So, no matter if you believe in God or don't, I do hope you try reading through the steps.)

What I found so challenging at first is to look at life from a different perspective and to work the steps. Some of the hardest (step 9: making amends to people you have wronged) can seem overwhelming at first. But the beauty of the Twelve Steps is that you don't have to do them all at once. Typically, you'll start at one, work your way through, fall back down to one, and then onward and upward again. You work them at your own pace.

When I look back at my first few Adult Children of Alcoholics Anonymous meetings, I felt so happy to have found other people who understood me and did not judge. And my sponsor was such a kind and patient man. After we had known each other for a while, we'd end our sessions with a hug. But he'd say, "Don't give some a man hug." (He'd demonstrated by pounding on my back while giving a quick hug.)

Instead, he gave a normal hug that was authentic and meaningful.

As a boy, I didn't have a male role model who gave me hugs. I'd get some quick ones from my grandfather, but he wasn't known for his affection. (Now as an adult, I make certain that I give hugs to both of my children.)

I remember how lost I felt back before I went to a therapist or had started the Twelve Steps.

And I look back now and see all that I've learned but understand the need to continue to grow and put effort into becoming a better person.

It's the same sort of work one does with a relationship. Marriages or long-term relationships take work. Listening, spending time together, talking, etc. Taking control of your life from having lived in an alcoholic/dysfunctional family also takes work.

I look at this way: To be fully present in a relationship, I must work on myself. I need to take care of "me" before I can take care of "us."

I'm a big proponent of Brené Brown's work. I've seen how she's risen to be a powerful force for good. But what I didn't know is that she had a drinking problem. More than 20 years ago, she stopped drinking and smoking. I don't know if she follows the Twelve Steps or not, but if you've not read any of her books, I highly recommend them.

Her book *The Gifts of Imperfection: Let Go of Who You Think You're Supposed to Be and Embrace Who You Are* is a great place to start. What I like about Brown's work is that she is not only relatable, but her books are accessible and helpful. There are dozens upon dozens of people that you read and get help from, but I trust Brown.

And if you have Netflix, be sure to watch her show *Call to Courage*.

What I learned is that I am not alone. Many people have struggled with overcoming their dysfunctional upbringings. Repeating patterns of destructive behavior in relationships, walling themselves off from love, being unable (or unwilling) to trust others—the list goes on and on.

If you want to take control of your life and be free, I remember how overwhelming it all felt. But, as with any path, the first step is only deciding to start and then putting one foot in front of the other.

You are not alone. There are so many great people in the world who can support and love you. I hope you see that.

DAY 15: OVERCOMING FEAR

I remember lying in bed and being afraid. I wasn't certain what the next day would bring. My brain spun in circles and recycled thoughts of worry, concern, and things that I just could not know.

I've had to face fear in my life, but I think one of the most complicated moments of fear I faced was when I met up with my father at my counselor's office.

After my father left my mom, brother, and me, I grew to hate my father. After about a year or so, he stopped coming to see me. I had this horrible feeling that he had written my brother and me off. He didn't care about us and I feared that he had moved on, having tossed us aside.

Over time my anger and hatred grew. The physical reminders of my father no longer existed in my world. Old photos had been blacked out. I had no physical reminder of my father.

But one Christmas, my family and I gathered around the projector and played our family movies from the old super 8 reel-to-reel. We projected the films onto a wall in my grandparents' house and watched the silent movies from years before.

During one film, I saw my mom running into the kitchen. I caught a glimpse of lit-up Christmas decorations, my grandmother standing over the stove cooking, and then a man sitting at a table. Young with a big smile, he turned toward the camera and waved. It was my father.

My Uncle, grandparents, and mom suddenly quieted from their usual commenting. The clicking sound of the film running through the projector filled the silence, and a few seconds later the scene shifted, and I sensed everyone breathing again.

That's how I grew up with the memory of my father.

As though he had the power to break through

the screen and come out like a modern-day horror villain to ruin all of our lives.

Fifteen years later, when I ran into his third wife by accident, my world had changed. I worked at a local department store, and when a woman that I waited on gave me her credit card to purchase the Christmas gifts that she wanted to buy, I paused. She had the same last name as me.

I chanced to ask her about it, and that's how I found out that she lived with my father no more than a mile from where we stood.

We met up for dinner a few weeks later, but the fear that I needed to overcome was so much bigger than a simple social gathering.

I asked my father if he would come to a counseling session with me. I didn't think he would, but he agreed.

So, on the way to my counselor, I had sweaty palms and had no idea how things would go.

I could have easily walked away and not faced my fear, but I had important questions that I need to ask. The most important of them:

Why?

That one word had more than 100 questions attached to it. But I would take as many of the "why" questions that I could ask in 50 minutes.

I don't remember what we said to each other when he arrived, but we walked in together, and my counselor did an amazing job in facilitating our conversation.

I learned an important lesson that day.

My father wasn't the demon I had made him out to be. He had done horrible things and had made bad decisions but was still human.

Now I had decisions of my own to make.

How would I choose to live my life? How would I overcome what I had been through? And most importantly, could I ever let go of my hate, anger, and fear?

That's a tall order.

A college professor once told me she had wished she had the opportunity to talk with her father about some of the bad things that happened in their family before he died. I took the chance to talk with my father and realized that the fear, anger, and hatred that had been cast over my life had crippled me.

To grow, I needed to let it go. I needed to find a way to deal with those emotions healthily.

I recently picked up Gay Hendricks' *Learning to Love Yourself*, and he shares a revolutionary idea.

When you are afraid, love that part of yourself.

If you're angry, think about why you're feeling angry and love yourself.

When hate is consuming you, reach inward and love that part of your inner self.

For so long, I tried to cut those pieces out of me. And failed.

I tried to rise above them and be better than them but failed.

Now that I am older and have more experience, I am learning to love those parts of myself.

It sounds so simple, but it can be hard.

Overcoming fear isn't about just facing it, but it's about loving the part of you that is afraid.

I wanted to write this today to remind myself of this important lesson as I need it today.

DAY 16: PREPARING FOR THE STRESS OF THE HOLIDAYS

As I write this, the holidays are right around the corner. And for those of us who grew up in an alcoholic/dysfunctional family, that's usually a trigger for anxiety and stress. What to do?

If you have a plan, then you'll be best prepared to handle anything that comes your way.

What I find to be extremely helpful is to be well-prepared. I do not like to leave things to the last minute around the holidays (that's the over responsible part of my growing up in a dysfunctional family coming out).

Keep in mind that there are only so many hours in the day and that you need to rest and have sleep. Running all the time to get everything done, will just tire you emotionally and psychologically.

For the holidays, I like to carve out time to:

- Read
- Listen to music
- Go for a walk or run
- Play games

Maybe some of the hobbies that I listed aren't for you and that's fine. Make certain that you carve some time out to take care of yourself.

Defend Your Boundaries

How often have you agreed to do something extra around the holidays? To help out a family member or friend? Work longer or harder to meet an end of the year deadline?

If you always say "yes," then it's important to set boundaries.

One of the easiest things to do is to turn your phone off.

Before we were attached at the hip with our phone, people would call us on our landline phones. And if we didn't want to answer, we let the message go right to voicemail.

These days with GPS tracking and texting, people can not only know exactly where you are but reach you in a second.

Stop that. Only a few people actually need to reach you so quickly.

By unplugging, you're not only setting a strong boundary but also giving yourself distance and space from the constant notifications that ping you incessantly throughout the day.

Leave your phone off more often around this time of year.

Make certain you treat yourself right (read, take a bath, listen to music, whatever helps you) and be sure to get the food and rest you need.

Running around constantly and being always on, will not only tire you out but it'll take the fun out of the holidays for you.

Prepare and be strong.

DAY 17: DON'T WORRY ABOUT IT: PYT (THE DANISH HAVE IT RIGHT)

You're rushing to meet the train and your heel breaks.

You're on the highway and get a flat tire.

You set your alarm to get up early, and the power goes out, and you oversleep.

Each day there are hundreds of little events that don't go our way. How do you handle stress events?

In my youth, I'd get upset and double-down trying to push on harder. I'd grit my teeth and push through to complete whatever I needed.

But there are events in life in which, things just happen. Sh*t happens. It just does.

How do you react to the situation?

Get upset and vent your anger? (That was my normal reaction.)

Or, why not practice "pyt" (an untranslatable Danish phrase that means "Don't worry about it" or "oh, well").

The Danish have learned that you'll have a much happier life if you learn to roll with the punches. Getting all emotionally invested on that glass of spilled milk on the carpet probably isn't going to solve the problem and your stress level only goes up.

But practicing pyt, might be worth checking out.

DAY 18: THE HEALING POWER OF PLAY

As a kid, I loved Lego. I could come up with an idea, grab my box of Lego and make anything I could dream up. Since I loved space, I have fond memories of building Lego spaceships and then driving around my neighborhood on my bike while "flying" my Lego spaceship.

Probably not the safest thing I could have done as a kid, but I didn't know any better.

I would sit in my living room and go through the cardboard box (an old Avon box as my mom was an Avon salesperson for many years) looking for that right piece. I can still hear the rattle of the Lego pieces in my memory. How my grandfather didn't want to banish me to another room is beyond me.

But playing, just for fun, became a way for me to deal with stress and anxiety. Building Lego spaceships also helped me socially as my friends and I had something in common that we could work on together.

We would act out the latest Star Wars movie with our Lego ships and pretend that we were off in a galaxy, far, far away.

Now I'm an adult, and playtime is considered only for kids.

As adults, we're supposed to like adult things or be too busy to play. However, I would disagree with those that knock the value of play. Without downtime, I think we miss out on the joy of reconnecting with ourselves and our friends.

If we only work, then that's a whole other sort of problem.

I challenge you to think about what you liked as a kid and see if you still can have fun with that.

Maybe that's collecting (stamps, vintage toys, etc.), building/creating (knitting, building models, etc.), making art (painting, sculpting, mudroom, etc.) or sports.

In our modern times, we're often too busy to

make time to play. I recommend that you challenge that.

Here are a few simple ideas that you can do that are a bit off the beaten path:

- Draw. Put on some music, grab some crayons, close your eyes, and just let your hand draw to the music. Art and music therapy are great ways to reconnect and have some downtime. My daughter recently asked my wife, her brother, and me to draw with our eyes closed to music, and I had a great time. Give it a try, and if you have kids, bring them into it as well. Have fun with it!
- Play a game together. I've talked about games that I've enjoyed, and there's a whole long list of fun games you can play. If you have more than three people, then you can play the card game Goop!. Or if you want to be more adventurous, I recommend cooperative games:
- Magic Maze: This board game is

simple. You're all trapped in a mall and need to get four items and then get to the exit. The only problem is that you can't speak to communicate during the game. You need to work together without words or pointing (ages 8+).
- Forbidden Island: You and your friends are all trapped on an island that's sinking. You need to work together to get various treasures and leave the island before it goes underwater.

What I like about cooperative games is that it's not the group fighting to see who is #1. Working together as a team is fun and takes some of the pressure out of play that might create conflict amongst a group.

If games aren't your thing, then explore your creative side. Coloring, cooking, canoeing, crafting, canning, camping—the list goes on.

Whatever you decide, be sure to have fun!

DAY 19: THE POWER OF SILENCE

We have TVs, car radios, our phones, and all sorts of other devices to play music, news, or live streams that block out our internal thoughts. I catch myself often in this trap.

I bring an iPad with me as I make and then eat my lunch. I might watch a YouTube channel, the news, a video podcast, or listen to music.

How often do we give ourselves the luxury of silence?

Probably not as often as what we used to do years ago.

When was the last time you had time to yourself to listen to your thoughts?

It is so easy not to give ourselves time to think

and just be. I know that I often push hard to finish work, get stuff done, and don't give myself time to reflect.

To be.

To sit in stillness and to embrace that moment. What would we think of during that time? How would we feel?

Maybe we don't give ourselves time to sit in silence because we're afraid.

Maybe it's time to face that fear and love that part of ourselves.

Just maybe, we might come out on the other side with a truer sense of who we are and what we want out of life.

For five minutes, sit alone in a room and turn off all sounds, notifications, and be with yourself.

How did that feel?

DAY 20: ACHIEVING HAPPINESS

What does it take to be happy? Is happiness directly tied to having lots of possessions, money, and fame?

Everyone's definition of what it means to be happy will be subjective, but I would like to put some thoughts out there.

Depression, anxiety, and stress can make finding happiness unattainable. We might even feel that we don't deserve to be happy, or are so overwhelmed, that we cannot imagine a way to allow ourselves to feel joy.

On a personal level, happiness has come to me at the times when I least search for it:

- Seeing my son and daughter playing a game together.
- Hearing my wife laughing in joy from something funny that a friend told her on the phone.
- Finishing a long run and realizing that I succeeded.
- Putting my thoughts down and publishing a book.
- Reading a good book and having the time just to relax.
- Watching the night sky and seeing a meteor streak across the sky.

For me, happiness is tied to my internal world. No matter what's happening in the world around you, if you're calm and okay within, you're still okay.

That's a powerful message if you stop to think about it.

There have been so many times in life that something has affected me from the outside and I crumble and immediately go into feeling gloomy instead of taking the time to separate my inner happiness with whatever is going on around me.

Sometimes life hits you hard with problem after problem and you might feel like you're Job from the bible.

But I've found that when I'm quiet, take time to relax and really just be, that this is when I'm most happy. In the examples that I shared above, there's a common thread. I'm sitting back and observing, thinking, and allowing myself to be present in the moment.

Choosing to be happy can be difficult.

There's a saying that we have in my family: "Don't let them get your goat."

When a person is trying to get a rise out of you or some unexpected news has hit you, we all have a choice to make. We can react or realize that we really are okay when everything is not okay. That might sound too simple of a decision. Granted, we've all had horrible news come our way: Death, sickness, loss of a job, and other big life events. I'm not saying that we ignore these life changing moments as each of them requires that we grieve and process what's happened to us in a different way.

But here's something to chew on: The Danish use the word "pyt" to describe a situation in which something unlucky happens to you, and you shrug it off. Pyt translates in English to something like:

"Don't worry about it" or "stuff happens." When a Danish person drops their ice cream cone on the ground, they say "pyt" and move on.

Imagine how powerful that would be if we were to take that to heart.

When I'm rushing to get the train, but I miss it: Pyt. I'm driving in my car and get a flat tire. Pyt. I send an article out to be published and get rejected: Pyt.

I've been working hard to incorporate the Danish response to simple frustrations into my life.

I can tell you that not only do I have less stress but I've also been happier.

When I merge the two thoughts together: "The world can be a maelstrom but I'm still okay" along with "stuff happens and time to let it roll off me," my worldview has changed.

Will these two ideas solve all my problems?

No.

But I'll tell you this: I've been a heck of a lot happier when I've allowed the little things to roll off my back and focus on surrounding myself with positivity.

Now, what about you? What makes you happy?

DAY 21: PROTECT YOURSELF AGAINST THOSE LASHING OUT

When I look back at the holidays over the years, I remember that there were certain family members in my life who knew how to get under other people's skin. Add in alcohol, dysfunction and put a bunch of people together and it's pretty much a recipe for disaster.

I've seen age-old feuds come out over family dinners and I've been pulled into being put in an uncomfortable position when a couple is broken up, and you're caught in the middle.

Through it all, one thing that's key is to focus on protecting yourself.

That might not be as easy as it might sound.

Sure, you can skip all the holiday festivities with your family, but that may not always be possible.

If you are at a family event and someone is trying to get a rise out of you (or drag you into an argument or start an argument with you), don't take the bait.

How easy it would be if we could simply always be able to handle the slings and arrows that come our way. But here's the thing that I find: I'm fine in protecting myself up to a point. I might even pat myself on the back in dealing with the passive-aggressive or outright hurtful comments being sent my way. Where I often fail is that I turn my frustration and anger on someone else.

Let's say that I'm at a party, and I successfully deal with three family members who are acting in their usual behavior, and I avoid the bait. But later, one of my kids might come up to me and do something to frustrate me, and that's the straw that breaks the camel's back.

I then get angry at my kid, feel guilty afterward, and need to apologize.

Have you seen yourself mimic that same behavior?

I'll go along and take, take, take, but then I can't take anymore and can get into an argument over the stupidest of things. I'm then embarrassed by that and feel shame and guilt.

I remember family members asking me as a kid what I wanted to be when I grew up. I'd tell them that I wanted to be a writer. They'd dismiss my answer and say: "You're tall. Why don't you want to play basketball?" Or, "You have good grades, be a lawyer or a doctor." It's those little jabs that I didn't know how to handle as a kid.

When I'd explain that I wanted to be a writer and loved it, they'd laugh it off and say that I should have a career that paid the bills.

Now, as an adult, I don't have to deal with the same sort of comments, but family members are always ready to judge: Over your political, religious, or career choices. Or who you are (or aren't) dating. And, my favorite, how you're raising your kids. Everyone's got an opinion. And brushing off the comments or telling people to mind their own business, does work, but there is also a need to have downtime to deal with your emotions and feelings.

I find it difficult to juggle so many things during the holidays. People's expectations, managing my own time with the added work on the home front and at work as well as making time to exercise, sleep, and meditate.

For me, I'm making healthy choices a priority (eating right, getting decent sleep, and exercise). But I'm also making certain that I work in time to relax and just chill.

When family members might make a difficult time for you during the holidays, remember to work on handling your own emotions or if you might just wind up lashing out on someone else.

DAY 22: THE COMPLEXITIES OF ALCOHOL

I have a love/hate relationship with alcohol. Many of my worst memories are around seeing people drinking too much. Family, friends, loved ones—alcohol is a trigger for me because it's a depressant that's so easy to abuse.

We have the wink-wink-nudge-nudge of how mommies need their little bit of red wine to get them through the day, and now they even sell "wine glasses" that hold an entire bottle of wine.

I grew up in an Italian family, and I could have a glass of wine with dinner if I wanted and remember trying a taste of scotch on the rocks when my great Uncles would come over for the holidays. The bitter taste would make my mouth pucker up, and I realized that I hated the taste.

After my mom divorced my father, alcohol took a backseat in my life. I had many years where fear of alcohol wasn't a thing for me. I'd only see alcohol being abused by adults during the holidays and at weddings.

But a strange thing happened when I became a teenager and went to college. Most of the people I knew were desperate for alcohol. It was the secret holy grail for them. I remember being in high school at a friend's house, and he went into his parents' liquor cabinet and stole a drink. He offered it to all of us, and my friends tried to peer pressure me into drinking. But I didn't want to. I could have a glass of wine any time I wanted at home, and I didn't want to drink.

As I grew older, my lack of interest in drinking made me even less popular. Not only was I a geek who liked fantasy books, but I also didn't like to party.

So, I went around to building my relationship with alcohol on my terms.

I've done my best to stay out of toxic alcoholic situations: New Year's Eve is always a tough one because people tend to drink too much, and I dislike being around sloppy drunks. I like to make certain that I have an exit plan so that I'm not trapped somewhere.

I've seen many friends and coworkers let loose because of alcohol, and I'd rather be me without needing the drink. If I want to have fun and sing on a table, I think we should do that because we want to and not because of the alcohol running through our system.

If you also have a complicated relationship with alcohol, I want to share a resource with you. Joy Manning, a former coworker of mine, has started the Better Without Booze website.

With the holidays upon us as I write this, there are some great non-alcoholic alternatives on her website. There are also some great resources.

I think Joy's bravery in starting her journey not to drink has inspired many to follow her.

If you're curious, I recommend checking her site out. And I don't know about you, but the Hibiscus Fizz looks good!

DAY 23: HOW TO DEAL WITH PEOPLE YOU DON'T WANT TO BE AROUND

Have you ever been in a situation in which you don't want to be around a particular person, but have to?

Might be family, work, or a friend's spouse, but we've all been in situations where the easiest thing to do would be to avoid the person like the plague.

Many years ago, when I first started in the workplace, I moved to a new department and had to deal with a difficult supervisor. I had a tough time working with this person. Two of my colleagues quit and found other jobs. It was a really difficult situation.

No matter how I tried to adapt and work with the person, they just made my life miserable.

Things got so bad that I started looking for a new job and wanted to leave as I couldn't handle the stress. But then an idea came to me. I met with the top boss and talked with them about how I felt.

The advice I was given: If I quit, then any time I came across a similar problem in the future, my instinct would be to run. I wouldn't know how to deal with the problem. Instead of letting the supervisor win and ruin my career, I could stay and hang in there.

I thought the advice to be solid but didn't know how long I could hold out. In my case, I got lucky because the top boss fired my supervisor a few weeks after we talked.

When I look back at this situation, I now realize a few things:

1. **No one can make you feel anything.** I allowed my supervisor to get to me and fell prey to their ego and dysfunctional work behavior. Next time

you're in a similar situation, remember that you are in charge of your feelings and not the person bothering you.

2. **Talk to someone.** In my case, I went right to the top, and that turned out to be the best course of action. The person who had power over my supervisor fixed the problem. Keeping all your feelings inside isn't going to make you feel any better. Talk to someone (people you trust), not to gossip but to learn how best to deal with the situation.

3. **Build up your boundaries.** What does this mean? If you don't get along with a family member, when you see that person, do your best to be civil and keep an emotional distance between you and the other person. Sure, you can try to heal a rift and forgive each other, but I've found that sometimes there are people who thrive on chaos and look to cause problems. Build up your boundaries and stay strong.

Let me talk a bit about boundaries. Bullies like to get reactions out of people. They prod, poke, and disturb to get people riled up. Don't fall for it.

That might be harder to put into practice than you might want. But what I find that works well, is the following response:

"I know that you're trying to upset me, but I'm not going to fall for it."

If your relationship with the person is more complicated than what you'd like, another good response is to redirect and focus on something different. Talk about another topic and refuse to engage in the conversation that is meant to trap or hurt you.

Being around someone that you don't want to can be challenging and emotionally draining. If it's someone you need to do daily, then I recommend that you work the following into your routine:

- Exercise (walking, running, whatever)
- Meditation (15-20 minutes a day can do wonders!)

- Get the proper amount of sleep.

At the end of the day, how you react to a situation is up to you. Being in the situation is challenging and can be toxic if you're not careful. Hopefully, these tips will help.

DAY 24: BEWARE OF ABSOLUTES (BLACK AND WHITE THINKING)

In growing up in an alcoholic/dysfunctional family, I learned to think in absolutes:

- Drinking alcohol was always bad.
- My father was also all bad.
- Dealing with a problem meant shutting someone bad out of your life —forever.

Shades of gray didn't exist. It was either one extreme or the other. The problem with thinking in absolutes is that life isn't like that, and sometimes I've missed out on the nuances in life.

Just because someone does a bad thing doesn't make them entirely evil and the devil. On the flip side, my mom went through hell in her first marriage, but she wasn't perfect (no one is).

As a kid, I had a skewed view of my parents. I idolized my mom as the suffering victim who did the best she could with what had happened to her. And for my father, I branded him as a demon and evil incarnate.

Growing up with such a limited view and living life that way put me in some tough situations. When I started dating and being in relationships, when bumps in the road came along, I often thought: "Well, this person is always a problem."

But what changed? As I grew up, I saw the world and realized all of us can make mistakes. And I know that I'm not all good or all bad. I am human and do the best that I can.

What's important isn't if I am perfect, but that I realize that after I make a mistake that I can atone for it and work to be a better person. And when I see others, and they make mistakes, to be open to listening to them and forgiveness.

The next time that you run up against a

problem and you catch yourself thinking that someone or something is all bad ask yourself: Is it true?

You might just be surprised by the answer that comes to you.

DAY 25: DEALING WITH FAILURE

I wrote my first story back in elementary school. It's a sci-fi story with aliens, the future, and a melding of what I had seen in *Blade Runner* and *Doctor Who*. I even drew cool little pictures of the aliens in the stories. From an early age, I knew that I wanted to be a writer. I found writing to be therapeutic and cathartic. Through my imagination, not only could I escape, but most importantly, I could deal with my feelings by playing scenes out among all the characters I created.

I wrote more stories, then wrote a novel at 16 and kept going.

I got my B.A. in English Literature and

French and then my Masters in English Literature.

I kept trying (and failing) to get my first novel published. I rewrote it, wrote other stories, but I eventually gave up.

Teacher after teacher kept telling me to find a day job because writing fiction didn't pay the bills. They were right, but only to a point.

I failed to achieve my dream of becoming a "famous" author. And when I hit rock bottom, I stopped writing fiction. I would blog or write non-fiction articles, but I gave up writing novels. I tried writing a sequel to my first book back in 1999, but the first draft still hasn't seen the light of day. I listened to what others said about writing and not being able to make a move and let failure win.

When we fail, it's like life is teaching us a lesson. The failure is giving us much-needed information on how to adapt, change, be flexible, but failure doesn't mean we suck or that we'll never succeed.

After my daughter came into the world, I had an idea to write a brand-new series based on Cinderella. The premise was simple: What happened after Cinderella married the prince? What if things weren't all happy ever after? Now ten years later, I have published 11 novels.

But I still haven't found a way to make a living off of my writing, but that doesn't mean that I have given up.

I have taken my failures and learned from them. I have become a better writer than I was ten years ago. If we allow failure to define us, to beat us down, and never to try, then we're allowing ourselves to be victims.

And I don't like that.

I'm a survivor.

I work hard and write because it's what I love to do.

Can my books be better? Yes.

But the only way I know how to become better is to read, listen to what other authors do and to learn from them and writing. I decided a long time ago that I would rather fail and see my failures than never to have tried.

At least from the ashes of failure, I can rise and build something newer and better. To be beaten down and trapped by failure is a prison to me.

What have you failed at? Marriage? A job? A childhood dream? Maybe you may not be able to become a super famous singer, but that doesn't mean you can't sing. Perhaps you can teach music or write books about music or sing in a choir, and though you might not believe it, maybe you can achieve that dream you had. The thing is—if you don't try and let failure define you, you'll never know.

So, what are you waiting for?

DAY 26: BEING THANKFUL FOR TODAY

It can be hard to be thankful for where we are today. We might be suffering and going through a difficult time. I know that in growing up, I often looked to the future, hoping that I would get to better days.

The problem with always looking forward is that I wasn't taking the time to be thankful for what I had around me and for the people in my life today.

When you grow up in an alcoholic/dysfunctional family, it's hard not to want to insulate yourself from hurt and hard times.

But if our defenses are always up, then we

can't let people in. We can't experience love, joy, and laughter.

Today I want to be thankful for where I am and all the wonder I have in my life.

I will always have struggles and challenges, but I want to focus on the positive today.

I'm thankful for my family, friends, and for all that I have been given.

Today I want to give myself the gift of relaxation. The gift to have fun and to not work. A gift to smile at those I love and to thank them for being in my life.

If you are struggling and going through a difficult time, I am sending you some happiness and joy. I cannot take your hard times away, but I hope that you know that you are never alone.

I wish you peace, health, and happiness.

Can you offer those same things to yourself?

DAY 27: BE TRUE TO YOURSELF IN THE NEW YEAR

When I write this, the new year is right around the corner. When I look back at the past and see where I have been, I'm amazed at how much I've learned, where I've been and how I've grown. I've also seen a lot of "end of the decade" articles on the web these days. We're getting ready to move into the next decade (yes, I know that some people believe the next decade doesn't start until 2021), and there is a lot to look forward to.

I'm taking the rest of this week to reflect on what I want in the next year (and beyond).

Are you taking time to reflect and get in touch with your feelings, what you really want, and how to embrace that moving forward?

During the winter holidays, I am often trying to cram in family and friend time, writing, reading, and watching movies, but taking time to reflect, meditate and plan out what I'd like in the upcoming year, not so much.

But this year is different because I am choosing to plan differently.

I have carved out time to reflect on my year-end author business blog post (for the last several years, I write about how much I've learned about the publishing business), but I'm also making time to focus on self-care activities:

- Journal writing
- Meditation
- Exercise
- Just having fun

When the new year starts, I want to make certain that I'm making time for activities and play that will be good for me. I am also working to ensure that I'm not brought into any family or work drama.

If you're dealing with some difficult life problems, maybe you can create new pathways for yourself?

- See a counselor/therapist.
- Read some self-help books.
- Join an online (and safe) community.
- Treat yourself (eat, sleep and rest)

I know that sometimes life gets in the way and we don't have the luxury to spend time or money on ourselves. But I would counter that with a small amount of time each day can make a big difference in your self-esteem and mental well-being.

Here are some ideas to help you:

- Practice yoga. Yoga with Adriene is a free YouTube channel. She has more than 5 million subscribers and I swear by her episode on the lower back. Treat yourself and try some of the beginning episodes.

- Watch Deepak Chopra's "The Healing Self" video on YouTube.

These suggestions are free and you can watch at your leisure.

Finding joy and peace in your life might take time, but you can do it. Changing one's habits and surrounding yourself with positive influences and healthy living does take time, but I know you can do it.

How?

One day at a time.

DAY 28: WITHDRAWING AS A COPING MECHANISM

Back in college, my Communications' professor had us take part in an experiment. She lined us all up in an empty classroom and told us to act funky and goofy as a way of representing different ways people interacted in a dysfunctional family.

Some of my classmates spun in circles, one walked funny, and another talked in a weird voice as she stomped across the room.

On seeing how everyone started to act, I chose to walk away from the group toward the opposite side of the room.

When our professor saw me doing that, she stopped everyone and asked me to share with the class why I had left the group.

At first, I thought I had done something wrong, but I told the truth: While growing up in a multi-generational dysfunctional family (Grandparents, siblings, parent, and children), I'd often withdraw into my creative little world when I couldn't take the problem du jour.

I still remember an all-out screaming match between my grandfather and grandmother over a bottle of Tylenol. Why they argued so much over something so insignificant is a whole other story.

Even before I lived with my grandparents, I went through some rough times during my mom's second marriage. But I had my books and still credit Dungeons & Dragons for allowing me to get through the worst of the times.

I shared with my class that my instinct is to walk away from the dysfunctional and do my own thing. At the time, I found this to be a healthy way of not dealing with drama. I simply would walk away.

However, now that I'm older, I've found that there have been times in the workplace where there has been dysfunctional behavior taking place (yelling, passive-aggressive behavior, lying, etc.), and my instinct is to avoid the situation like the plague. While that worked well as a kid, that's not always helpful in either a relationship or at work.

I've learned that there is a healthy balance. The adult child of an alcoholic and dysfunctional family part of me wants to withdraw to be safe. That's why I walked off during the classroom experiment.

The challenge is finding a way to deal with difficult situations when your instinct is to run.

Create Safety

In a recent keynote speech that I heard at Project Management Institute's global conference; Adam Grant shared five tips on having more successful projects. You might think what this has to do with relationships, but here's how he framed it:

No matter if we're at work, school, or at home, we all want the same thing: We want to feel safe and trusted.

Grant urged people to create a safe psychological environment to have more successful projects.

That makes a lot of sense to me. At work, no one wants a boss to yell at them or to be punished for speaking up. He gave a powerful example: During a high-level meeting, the CEO of a company gave a bad pitch presentation to a potential client. A lower-level employee wrote to the CEO and told him that. The amazing thing is that instead of becoming defensive and aggressive, the CEO forwarded the email to the entire company and owned up to having dropped the ball.

The CEO took responsibility for his mistakes and vowed to do better.

The same type of behavior can be applied to your relationships. We all make mistakes. The challenge is to create an environment that's safe to fail. None of us is perfect. Imagine having a safe environment to discuss difficult topics and where people owned up to their mistakes. How often in a relationship do the defenses come up, and it's "my side" versus "their side"?

The Changing Dynamics of a Dysfunctional Family

But if you live in an environment where there isn't psychological safety, trying to convince someone to work with you might not work. The same is true at your job. If people aren't willing to change the culture and create psychological safety, that's not going to help you.

When I feel threatened, my two modes of operation are:

- Put on a strong offense to defend myself.
- Withdraw to protect myself.

But imagine the power in living in a safe psychological environment and one in which participants are open, honest, and inviting.

The rules for safe arguing need to agree upon in advance. When someone hits their limit, they can tap out to take some time to regroup and think about their next steps.

With dysfunctional environments, as soon as one person either leaves or changes how they react to a situation, the entire group is affected.

For a dysfunctional family, that will offset everything. It's like a baby mobile hanging over a crib if you pull on one string, the entire mobile shifts and moves.

Coming Out of the Shell

Withdrawing from conflict or a tough situation has helped me, but it's also hindered my grow at times. What I have been working on is building a safe environment in all my relationships. The challenge is having other people work with you. If there's fear in any of those environments that's a motivation to people in the group (let's say that a boss will flip out if you make a mistake), it's going to be harder to fix that environment.

However, if all parties agree to work on changing, great things are possible.

For me, I'm working on what I can change in myself. That starts with not running off emotionally any time there's a problem that comes up. I still need time to process big problems and decisions, but I am working to come back to express how I feel, what my thoughts are, and on listening.

I wish I could say that all of this is easy, but it's not. Still, the more that we're aware about ourselves, the better.

My purpose in writing is to share the problems I've encountered from having grown up in a dysfunctional family (due to emotional abuse, drugs, and alcohol). Who I am is directly affected by that, and it's shaped how I respond to different types of problems. The hurt and fear are real and hard to work through.

But the biggest thing is overcoming the shame that I've felt over the years. I'm different, but I've learned that's okay.

For me, a big step is being vulnerable. Sharing my story and being honest. If you've never seen Brené Brown's TED talk on the Power of Vulnerability, go check it out. It'll change your world.

DAY 29: THE F WORD: FORGIVENESS

The pain of the past can be hard to overcome. Your pain is yours and may have been inflicted on you by a family member or spouse. What I've seen over the years is the heaviness and internal struggle that people have carried with them for years.

Forgiveness is not easy to do, but as part of the first step, I ask if you could forgive yourself.

I look back at my childhood and all that my mom suffered. When my brother and I grew older, my mom often came to us and apologized for all that we had to live through. She felt guilty that she couldn't always protect or provide us with what we needed.

And I know that it's been hard for her to forgive herself. Choosing a partner who treated her badly, is a weight that my mom carried with her for a long, long time.

But the destructiveness of alcoholism and dysfunctional patterns is that the behavior that we see tends to be generational. Adult children of alcoholics often find themselves in similar relationships.

I grew up thinking that my partner and I would be together forever and that we would help each other become whole. Two halves would become one. The fallacy in that thinking is clear for anyone to see. But it took me years and years to figure that out.

Worse, it took me a long time to forgive myself.

The complexities of having grown up in an alcoholic/dysfunctional family is two-fold: I've chosen to be with partners who were not emotionally able to be there for me and then I took my frustration and resentment out on them. My behavior perpetuated the cycle of anger (be sure to check out the book *The Dance of Anger* if you're looking to understand more on this topic), and no matter how hard I tried to solve my problems, the more I found myself deep in misery.

How did I get out of this?

A therapist and following the Twelve Steps.

And then I learned how to forgive myself. It took time, lots of time, but I realized that I needed to let go of my shame and work on learning behaviors that would be helpful to my family and to me.

Today I wanted to focus on forgiving ourselves because it's important that we start there.

If you're going through a difficult time, what can you do to ease up on yourself and begin to forgive?

Admitting that you have a problem now (no matter the issue), is the best time to start dealing with your challenges.

A big part of that is forgiveness.

DAY 30: SERIOUSLY, MAKE TIME TO HAVE FUN

When I do get time off, I often make time to do work. Sure, it's work for me: Writing books, blog posts, newsletters, research or whatever, but then I get frustrated that my time off is over and I have to go back to my normal day-to-day.

If you're busy with work, family life or just stressed out, here are a few simple things you can do:

- If the weather's warm, start a water balloon fight.
- Have children? Allow them to try and tickle you and try not to laugh.

- Play charades.
- Grab a deck of cards and play thirty-one.
- Learn to paint.
- Sing songs while dancing around the house.
- Play a board game. (My family and I still play the board game Parcheesi and have a great time with the kids.)
- Teach your kids how to plant a vegetable garden.
- Start a book club with a few friends.

If you're not up for hanging out with people and just want some alone time, then there are a lot of great things you can do to have fun:

- Write a book.
- Start a journal.
- Read a book.
- Sketch or draw.
- Take a walk or run.
- Listen to music.

- Meditate.
- Go for a nap.
- Take a bubble bath.
- Get a massage.
- Go to a quiet place, find a secluded spot and just sit. (Let your mind wander and be free.)
- If you're on the east coast in the United States, go visit Longwood Gardens (and be sure to walk all through the meadow where there aren't many people).

Now I'm going to follow my own advice. I need to go have some fun. Life has been a bit stressful and I'm looking to unwind and just relax.

Hope these tips help you.

DAY 31: EVEN IN DARKNESS PERSEVERE AND CLING TO HOPE (THE POWER OF CREATIVITY)

We took our kids to see Greta Gerwig's new version of *Little Women*, and I had to come home to write. If you have not seen the new movie, I urge you to see it. If at the very least, be sure to watch the trailer. Gerwig's version is unique, fresh, and gets to the heart of the story—what can a woman do to make her way in the world if she doesn't marry?

Although Louisa May Alcott wrote *Little Women* 150 years ago, her book (and Gerwig's modern take) is still as powerful today.

We, humans, have the power to use our imagination and life experiences, capture them in words, and then share our art with the world.

No matter the hardships and pain that we go through, we have art to transcend, and those stories can help heal us.

Think about that for a moment.

Louisa May Alcott died in 1888, but her work is still influencing people today. The written word can transcend time, wars, and even death. What she felt and thought has been captured in a book that's been made into many different films over the years.

I wonder if Louisa May Alcott imagined that one day women would have the right to vote, or serve in the army, be a CEO and even be the leader of some of the world's most powerful countries.

The world has changed from Alcott's time and will continue to improve. I hope and pray that my daughter (and hopefully both my son's and daughter's future children) will see more equitable options made available for women.

There is a lot of darkness in our world. Famine, greed, death, corruption—the list goes on, but we have a choice.

How we grew up and how we choose to live can be entirely different.

Twenty-five years ago, my wife and I took our

first vacation together through the New England states. We stopped, and I made etchings of Emerson's, Thoreau's, and Louisa May Alcott's tombs. As the first in my family to go to college, I chose to be an English Literature major because I wanted to write and share my stories with the world.

I respected Alcott's hard work and made an etching of her grave to remind myself of the struggle she went through to publish her work as a woman.

And today, I sat in a movie theater with my children to watch *Little Women*.

There is no way that my teenage self could ever imagine that I deserved to fall in love, marry, and raise a family with my life.

When you grow up in an alcoholic/dysfunctional family, you just try to survive. I had no idea where I would be, how I would survive, and what I ever would grow up to do. I couldn't see it because my world centered around the dysfunctional behavior.

The shame of having a father who abused my mom. The pain of being the son of a man who did such things, and I had his blood in me. And the brokenness I felt in being lost and alone as I could not find a way to be deal with it all. I kept seeing other families be happy, but I didn't know how to do that. I only knew what I grew up around and how my experiences affected me.

I know that someone will eventually find this passage and read it in the depths of despair. I understand what that feels like.

If I could go back in time to my past self, I would tell him not to give up. To love himself with as much passion and joy as he could muster and that the shame and anger and hurt would fade away if he loved himself.

One day he would be happy. One day he would have a family and need to pass on to his children what he learned.

The power of Louisa May Alcott's work is that it's timeless. I feel for the sisters because they come alive on the page and in the movies.

Art can save and heal you. That is what I would tell my teenage self. The power of a book or a movie can be what helps you transcend the darkness you're dealing with and inspire you to get help, and not give up.

All my life I have tried so hard to not be like my father. I have struggled to get to where I am, but the secret of it all is in the quiet moments of life.

To stop and love yourself.

Alcott knew something about hardship and how to overcome them. Gerwig picks up that thread with a modern slant and directs a powerful scene in the movie. When all seems lost, and no one is around you, what will you choose to do?

Will you give in to defeat?

Or will you rise up and still persevere?

I am so happy that my teenage self chose to persevere.

And dear reader, if I could take your hands in mine, I would look you in the eye and tell you not to give up. Please, you are not alone. You are loved. **You just are.**

DAY 32: HOW TO AVOID ALWAYS THINKING THE WORST

Growing up in an alcoholic and dysfunctional household, I learned quickly that bad things happened a lot. To overcome those horrible times, I began to prepare for them. What I could anticipate, I would adapt, avoid, and survive.

Anticipation and preparation for challenging problems is a great life skill when you're in a crisis, but always thinking the worst can become a handicap in how to view life.

When I became a young adult, I still chose to see the world as a series of pitfalls that I had to prepare for. If a girlfriend didn't call me, I imagined the worst (she had cheated or want to leave me).

My friends never seemed to have this cloud of worry over them. They grew up in stable homes and knew that their foundations were strong. But for me, I lived life always ready for the rug to be pulled out from under me. As a kid, we moved four times, and I went to five schools from kindergarten through high school, and my mom went through two divorces.

I didn't know when the next move would take place or when I'd be involved in more family drama.

Since my upbringing was chaotic, my relationships mirrored that pattern.

What I realized in my 20s is that I had to find a way to stabilize my life. I couldn't keep chasing after ghosts of the past and repeating dysfunctional behavior.

If I always looked for the worst in everything, then I'd be limiting myself and creating an environment to self-sabotage my relationships. Always thinking the worst is draining and emotionally destructive for your partner.

To stop that behavior (and let me be clear, when I'm beaten down and weak, I still have to wrestle with these thoughts—you might not want to hear that, but it's not like there's a magical "cure" to take all those negative thoughts away), I have a few go-to activities:

- Focus on self-care (good rest, exercise, and eating).
- Love yourself. If I don't love me and feel strong in my own inner world, I can't be there for others.
- Meditate. When stressed out, meditation helps calm me.
- Self-reflection. I ask myself: Is it true? (Is it true that the worst is about to happen? Is it true that [fill in the blank]?)

Overcoming negative thoughts and thinking the worst is happening (or will happen) can be nearly impossible in the moment. But I found some solid tips that have helped me break the cycle of ruminative thoughts.

The challenge might seem overwhelming, but the good news is that you don't have to do all the work at once. Like most things in life, it'll take time and patience.

One step at a time.

DAY 33: AN ENDING IS A NEW BEGINNING

As I write this, New Year's Eve is finally here. And 2019 has been a rough one for many reasons.

I'm looking forward to 2020 and the new decade.

I've learned a lot in the last ten years and have seen such a significant change. At the beginning of the decade, my kids were both so little! I've learned a lot as a parent in ten years, and I will say that one of the most important things that I've learned is how to admit when I'm wrong with my kids.

Growing up, I always wanted my father to come back and say that he not only apologized for all that he had done to our family, but I wanted him to admit that he was wrong.

Hearing an adult say, "I screwed up, I made a mistake," and then actively work to be better would have been amazing.

Still, I'm not blinded by what happened. Even though my mom and father divorced more than forty years ago, she still doesn't like people to apologize to her. Why? She's sick of hearing people make apologies but never change their behavior. Her opinion is that actions speak louder than words.

With my kids, when I make a mistake or fail at something, I go and talk with then. I let them know that I was wrong or share how I failed. But what's most important is that I then tell them what I'm going to do to overcome the failure or how I'll work on being a better person.

Then I take making that change to heart and work (and be sure to show them by example) on solving the issue or showing them how I am working to be better.

I've always treated my kids as individuals — they have their own personalities and are not an extension of me. When either of them asks me the question: "What should I do?" or "What should I pick?" I throw the question back at them: "What would you like to do or pick?"

And so, we're at the ending of a decade in which now I see a great change in the world. Each of us has a choice every single day.

I choose to work toward being good and helping others. Like Paulo Coelho's manual *Warrior of the Light*, I strive to bring goodness to the world. If you're not familiar with Coelho's work, please pick up *The Alchemist*. He has sold more than 165 million books worldwide, and *The Alchemist* is a great fable about self-discovery.

With 2020 only hours away, I am committed to continuing my journey of self-discovery and working to help others.

Although the end of a year and the decade is upon us, there's a new beginning. When one door shuts, another opens.

And when the new door does open, what will you do?

DAY 34: PUSHING YOURSELF TOO HARD

As I write this, I'm fighting off a nasty cold. When I get sick, I get frustrated because I keep trying to push myself hard to write, read, and do work.

But you know what?

Resting would be the best thing.

But I have always pushed myself hard and held myself to a high standard. I've taken the mantle of responsibility that grew out of my childhood and ran with that.

My mom and family often told me after my father left, "you're the man of the family now," and the expectations weighed hard on me. I wasn't given any rules on how to be "the man of the house," so I interpreted that to mean that I worked hard, stayed in line with being a good kid, and was always mindful of the tough time around me.

Here is a reminder for you:

It is okay to rest. It is okay to relax and take care of yourself when you're sick. Remember that.

And with that said, I need to do the same and rest up so that I feel better.

Peace.

DAY 35: NEW YEAR, NEW ATTITUDE AND NEW HOPE

For me New Year's has come and gone, and now we're full-on into 2020. All the hubbub of the holidays are past, and I'm starting to get back into my normal daily routine with work, school, and family life.

I had a tumultuous 2019, and I want to be positive for 2020.

About halfway through 2019, I decided to focus on activities that would be helpful to me on my journey.

I exercise regularly, meditate daily, and have loaded up podcasts and books to help me learn better behaviors and on how to practice being a better person.

Many years ago, I chose to incorporate the Twelve Steps of Adult Children of Alcoholics into my life. If you're not interested in the Twelve Steps, then whatever works for you to help you with dealing with your past trauma—go for it! (Therapy, yoga, meditation, reading, etc.)

I look at things this way: When I wanted to learn how to run a marathon, I followed a training plan. I didn't wake up one day and say, "I think today I'm going to run a marathon." I had two years of running under my belt before I started a training program that got me to the 26.2 miles. It was hard work, but I'll share this:

In anything that I've had to accomplish in life, there are no shortcuts.

And looking back, the work I undertook along the way helped me learn what I needed to achieve my goal. I've written novels, created podcasts, run half and full marathons—all of these accomplishments took effort, perseverance, and hard work.

And there's nothing wrong with that.

When I am up against a difficult challenge, I make certain that I break up the goal into smaller chunks. Writing 1,000 words four times a week over several months is a lot easier to do than to say: "I want to write a book, but I don't know where to start." Or even worse, to start on a journey but give up because the goal hasn't been clearly defined.

If you want to make changes in your life, what I've found that works for me is starting small. I also surround myself with positivity. The shows I watch, the podcasts I listen to, the music I dance to when I'm beaten down, and the books that I read.

I believe in the power of a support network around me.

By building up a positive support group around me, I have people in my life who can help support me when I need someone to listen to me, and I've built out playlists and activities to help me.

Some of them you might laugh at: When I'm really in a sour mood and exhausted, then I know I need to sleep. Other times I go for a walk or a run. Or meditate or listen to *The Beatles* (or other uplifting music).

Start small and then build.

Build a strong foundation and then expand from there.

I know you can do it!

DAY 36: MAKE TIME FOR FUN

I'm a hard worker. I take on lots of responsibility. I get up early to write novels (or this blog), I've trained for marathons, and you know what? Only working is detrimental to my well-being. Always being on the go and never stopping to have fun not only isn't healthy, but it makes me a party pooper! Here are some ways to overcome that.

Make Time for Fun

Each spring, my family and I have a "pink confetti party." We have a cherry blossom tree on our front lawn and invite some friends over for a barbecue. We'll get everyone on the front lawn, we share something that we're happy about and then shake the tree so that the cherry blossoms fall all over everyone.

It's a lot of fun.

Over the years, we've added some fun things to the party. My favorite is buying some color powder packs, giving out white t-shirts, and then having a free-for-all color fight.

We got the idea of doing the color powder packs after having participated in a 5K Color Run a few years back. Thousands of people came out for the race, and at the end, you have a color powder fight with thousands of people. Not only did the kids have a blast, but my wife and I did as well.

Games, Games and More Games

I love playing games. Growing up, I played Dungeons & Dragons, Atari video games and lots of board games (Clue, Monopoly, etc.). Now that are kids are older, we can finally play more complex games (not that there's anything wrong with Candyland, but I did get tired of it).

If you're looking for a great game to play with friends or family, I highly recommend Settlers of

Catan. I love that game and there are lots of expansions with it. You try to build settlements on a map and trade with players for resources (sheep, wheat, ore, wood, and brick).

You'll have hours of fun over the years in playing the game—though you might get into some tense battles over people who refuse to trade with you. Personality clashes might happen, so be warned!

If you don't have a lot of money or want to play a game right now, then give the card game Goop! A try. Many, many years ago (the article I wrote about the game is from 2002), friends of ours taught us this card game. The best way I can describe it is by saying that it's like solitaire that you play with other people. All you need are at least four people and a deck of cards for each person.

Get Outside and Enjoy

If games and throwing a party isn't your thing, then why not get outside. Being an introvert, I find that running on my own is a great way for me to deal with stress and my problems. I run without music and like to enjoy nature. The good news is that the sport is inexpensive. All you need are some good running sneakers (seriously, be sure to get fitted at a store so that you get the right type of sneaker. If you're serious about running, get a half size larger than normal as your feet swell during a long run), comfortable running clothes, and that's it.

And if you're not into running, then go for a long walk. I love walking on a beach or going for a hike. If you can't get away from the city, then just get out and walk. I recommend bringing no music with you and keeping your phone off. Sometimes fun doesn't have to be loud and with other people. Enjoying yourself can be simply that—spending time with your thoughts and enjoying the world around you.

Read and Sneak in a Nap

Grab a book and read. Or better yet, write books like I do. For me, there's nothing better than going to read up in bed. I'll tell my kids that I'm "going to read" and I'll do so for a few minutes and then take a nap. Since I am up so early each day, a nice 20-30-minute nap in the middle of the day not only makes me less cranky, but I get to chill out and relax.

Nearly a quarter of Americans don't read books. I find that to be amazing. Still, reading isn't for everyone. But if you're not really into reading books, then I'd recommend trying out an audiobook. If you don't have time to read, then you can do other things while listening.

Spontaneous Fun

In need of some ideas, to help you have some fun? Start a spontaneous water fight in the summer or have an indoor "snowball" fight (with fake snowballs) if it's cold outside.

Play charades with your friends. Or if it's just your adult friends hanging out, take the cards from Cards Against Humanity and play Pictionary with them (seriously, Cards Against Humanity is not for the timid and definitely not for kids).

Or one of my favorite times I've had is having friends over and breaking up into two teams and holding an Iron Chef-like cook-off. You'll have a lot of fun with friends, and it'll be a blast.

There are so many things to do to have fun. If

we work so hard and don't take time to relax, then we'll just be miserable.

So, take some time to play with your kids or your family. No matter if it's a card or video game, cooking together, or spending time on your own to watch a movie or going on a bike ride, there's a whole range of fun activities to take part in.

What are you waiting for?

DAY 37: HOLDING A GRUDGE

I held onto my hatred and anger at my father for more than twenty years. I wrote him off until our paths crossed more than twenty years ago. What I realized is that holding a grudge over someone can make us feel powerful when we had no power in the past.

But that anger eats you up and is a convenient way of not dealing with your feelings.

How much easier it was to just write off my father because of the past then it was to deal with how I felt inside.

Over time, you can use the grudge as a crutch for many different things: Boost you up to feel strong, fuel you to get through a difficult time, deflect uncomfortable feelings onto your memory of a past event—even if that past is not relevant to your present.

Forgiveness is never easy when pain and suffering are wrapped around your memories of how someone treated you.

Blaming others and holding a grudge are the easy way out.

But what's more complicated is looking at how you were hurt, working through that (with a therapist if necessary) and coming to terms with forgiving the person.

Forgiveness is a double-sided coin. Yes, the act of forgiving can help the person who wrong you, but it also is a means for you to offload the anger and hurt feelings that you lived through.

What's complicated in an alcoholic and dysfunctional home is that you might learn that the person who mistreated you is also part of the generational effects of alcoholism or addiction. No, that doesn't absolve the person for mistreating you, but it does help put the situation in context.

Choosing to break out of the cycle and work on self-care and healing, is a much more productive way of moving forward in life than holding that grudge.

Is it easier to work through the pain and change your behaviors to live a healthier life? No, honestly, it's not.

But the alternative is carrying a lump of coal-fire in your heart all through your life and that anger and hatred are going to come out in ways that you might regret.

Learning to let go is hard, but healing.

DAY 38: THE POWER OF MINDFULNESS

I made a conscious decision halfway through 2019 to focus on mindfulness. I noticed that my behaviors were not aligning with my desire to be at peace and ease.

Instead, I rushed around a lot, struggled with stress and anxiety, and had a difficult time with sleep.

To change that, I turned to meditation, yoga, and mindfulness.

It's funny that what has worked best for me to deal with stress and anxiety is what I least wanted to do. I kept thinking: "I don't have time for that."

I kept worrying, and I felt worse and worse.

Finally, I decided to make a change. I focused

on techniques to help me stop worrying and deal with my anxiety.

I made time in my day and set up a pretty simple schedule. Every morning before work (and on the weekends), I would make time for 15-20 minutes to meditate.

What's worked for me are guided sessions by Deepak Chopra and Oprah.

But if that's not your thing, then I have found the following visual technique to be extremely helpful:

Sit down and relax. Close your eyes, and then slowly breathe in through your nose. As you're breathing, imagine warming and healing light entering your body that courses through your veins.

Then slowly exhale through your mouth while you imagine all the darkness and fear within you leaving your body.

Continue to slowly inhale and imagine the light slowly coursing its way through your body, hold your breath for a few moments and then again exhale slowly.

Keep relaxed, still, and keep your eyes closed.

If you would be more relaxed lying down in bed, then do so.

The purpose of the visualization technique is

to focus on your breathing, your body, and relaxing your mind.

I know that I rush through life and try to get so much done but I wasn't taking the time that I needed for self-care.

If you're stressed out, worried, and dealing with stress, anxiety, or ruminative thoughts, focusing on mindfulness will help.

DAY 39: SEE YOUR FLAWS AND QUIRKS FROM ANOTHER'S POINT-OF-VIEW

Sometimes a bit of helpful and objective information falls into my lap, but I'm not ready to understand and take the feedback.

Maybe that's because our first instinct is to be defensive. It's difficult to take feedback and to be open about it.

That's part of the reason why I like the fourth and sixth steps of Adult Children of Alcoholics:

"4. Made a searching and fearless moral inventory of ourselves."
 and:

"6. Were entirely ready to have God* remove all these defects of character."

(*Substitute "higher power" if the word God throws you off here.)

Taking an inventory of yourself and seeing your flaws, quirks, and imperfections can be helpful. Is it easy to do?

No, it's not.

What I've learned over the years is that to grow, I need to see my imperfections and become a better person. Growth takes time. Thankfully, I'm not the same person I was back in my 20s or 30s.

I've grown and learned how to handle different types of challenges and problems.

If you grew up in an alcoholic and dysfunctional family like me, our challenges are different than others.

The question I ask myself is: Do I want to grow or be stuck in perpetuating the unhealthy behaviors I learned as a kid?

I think what many people don't understand is that we might never have a problem with alcohol or drugs, but it's the behaviors we learned to cope with what we grew up with that we need to address.

Not sure what I'm talking about?

Read through the laundry list from the Adult Children of Alcoholics' website.

Yes, there's a lot to go through there. But if you read through the flip side of the laundry list, you'll also see that it's not a lost cause.

One of the first steps is overcoming denial and embracing acceptance.

If you feel overwhelmed and not sure where to start, that's okay. I'd recommend that you love yourself for feeling upset, confused, and maybe even angry.

Be good to yourself. If loving the icky parts of yourself is hard to do, then try reading Gay Hendricks' *Learning to Love Yourself* book. (If you have Amazon prime, the Kindle version of the book is currently free.) I read Hendricks' book recently, and the most inspiring part for me was reading through the scripts of people who were asked in the moment to love the parts of themselves that they didn't like. It might even sound counter-intuitive, but I recommend that you try it.

Remember, you're not alone. If you feel overwhelmed, reach out for help. There is no shame in admitting that you need assistance.

DAY 40: DEALING WITH MISPLACED ANGER

We all get angry at some point or another along the line. However, I've found that growing up in an alcoholic and dysfunctional family creates a special relationship between how we act and our anger.

If you need a refresher, first take a look at the laundry list from the Adult Children of Alcoholics' website.

Reading through the list can be difficult as it's like looking in the mirror and coming to terms with your own faults.

In my life, I've placed myself in situations in which I'm looking for a person to provide me with emotional and psychological support. I expect that a partner will be there for me as I will be there for them.

However, if the partner is unable to be there for me (due to their own struggles and inability to do so), then resentment and anger slowly buildup over time until the stupidest of things can set me off, and then I get angry at them.

The tricky thing is that sometimes the anger we feel is misdirected toward the wrong people.

Ever have a bad day at work and then come home and take it out on your kids or your spouse? That's a common one that I've seen many people do and I've been guilty of this behavior myself.

A long time ago, my first counselor once shared with me some words of wisdom. He passed on to me that the best way to deal with anger is to make certain that I take care of my basic needs:

- Ate when hungry.
- Slept when tired.
- Talk with a friend when lonely.

He also asked that I stopped and took the time to deal with my emotions when I became angry. Anger isn't necessarily a "bad" emotion; we just need to be careful that we understand why we're feeling that way and work on productive ways to deal with the anger.

I think back when my kids were little and they'd go through a tantrum about not getting something that they wanted. Rewarding that behavior only made things worse, but validating and listening to them on why they were angry and working with them on how they could deal with the emotions they were feeling was a much more positive way to help them learn some basic life skills.

As an adult who grew up in an alcoholic and dysfunctional family environment, the relationship we have with anger might be much more complex. We might have seen anger rewarded by having the person who screams, yells, or hits impose their power on others. Or we might have grown up with internalizing anger and taking out our emotions on ourselves with thinking we were too weak to handle a problem.

When in a difficult situation where I'm angry, I carve time out to take stock of my feelings, see if

I'm hungry, tired or lonely and then make certain that my basic needs are met first.

Afterward, I then think through why I'm feeling angry. Even if I believe that I am in the right, anger can be misplaced toward those who don't deserve it.

Some practical activities that I use to help me deal with anger are:

- **Write it out.** I sit down and write about why I'm angry. I don't censor myself. I simply write how I feel.
- **Ask a question.** "Is it true?" I like to ask myself this question to clarify who I'm angry at and then I also use the same question to help me think through my actions. Yelling at someone might make me feel better in the short-term but such a display of emotion might not solve the problem in the long run.
- **Stop the dance.** Anger can be cyclical and can branch out in many forms. Here's a classic example: A husband has a bad day at work. He

comes home and yells at his wife. She takes her anger out on the kids. The kids are angry at each other or internalize the anger and blame themselves. Rinse and repeat day after day and year after year, and you have a perfect example of the dance of anger that is perpetuated in many families. Be aware of this behavior and stop it.

To help break me out of my angry moods, there are some simple solutions:

- Try this yoga practice: fists of anger. (I tried this once and was wiped out from it. My anger just drained out of me.)
- If the fists of anger yoga practice is a bit much for you, trying dealing with anger with Yoga with Adriene on YouTube.

- And if yoga isn't your thing, go for a walk, a run or exercise.
- Listen to music to help you lift your mood.
- Talk with a close friend about your feelings (and how you can resolve the problem).

Dealing with misplaced anger can be challenging, but if you're aware that you're doing it and take steps to deal with your anger, you'll be well on your way to solving the problem.

DAY 41: CHOOSE GOOD FRIENDS

I have no way to go back in time and undo any of the mistakes I've made in my life. Because I grew up in an alcoholic and dysfunctional home, I took on behavior patterns that affected how I acted in relationships.

I found myself attached to people who I perceived as needing fixing and I'd try to "help them."

Even writing that sentence makes me cringe.

But I didn't know any better and acted like a fool. I never could help the people that I thought needed my help and eventually learned that I needed to take care of my own problems and let others handle theirs (in their own time).

I've had all sorts of friends and acquaintances over the years and have had to distance myself from some. The tricky thing is when you have decided to make a change in your life but those around you haven't. I'm remembering friends who just liked drinking and going out—all the time.

There's nothing more frustrating to be working on the issues you had with a family member who abused alcohol and your friends just do the same. I have had to distance myself from certain friends over the years because I needed to carve boundaries and a safe space for myself.

Now I'm more selective in who I spend my time with and open up to.

If you have a friend that tries to nudge you to act or say things that you don't really want to do or you're the punching bag for, maybe it's time to put some distance between the two of you.

I have had some friends that were extremely negative and liked to complain (though I must admit that I have done this myself at times). It's okay to question who you spend your time with and why.

It's also okay for you to be open to making new friends.

What's important is finding out what you want.

What do you want in a friend? And why?

To flip things a bit, I also think it's important to reflect on my own behavior. As a friend, have I been open-minded and made time for people in my life? Am I an active listener and willing to help?

Keep in mind the importance of having a few close friends in your life and being a good friend.

Both sides of the coin are invaluable.

DAY 42: EATING RIGHT

Each year I go to my doctor for my checkup, and she tells me to make certain that I eat right and take care of myself (both physically and mentally). I like the yearly check-in with my doctor.

When I was a kid, there were times that my mom didn't have healthcare for my brother and me. I remember going to the neighborhood doctor only when we were deathly sick. Back then, the doctor would give you a little shot to make you feel better. Who knows what was in that.

And since we didn't have healthcare, I didn't have regular checkups at the dentist. When I did have a problem (I needed braces), my mom took us to a local clinic. We waited in long lines, but I did get descent dental care.

Back in the '80s, I drank soda like that it was water and had candy and sweets like all the other kids.

But now I'm an adult and I'm responsible for my own choices.

You might wonder what diet has to do with growing up in an alcoholic and dysfunctional family.

Because I'm an over-achiever, I used to have tons of caffeine to keep me going. In graduate school, I would stay up until sunrise and would have pitchers of Cherry Coke.

What was I thinking? Who knows?

In the '80s and '90s, most of my friends and some family members smoked. Between the second-hand smoke and all the caffeine and sugar that I had in me, I'm surprised that I made it where I am now.

Once I became an adult, I noticed a direct connection between my moods: If I had lots of sugar, I'd feel great for a bit but then crash quickly. Caffeine had the same effect on me. I'd feel wired for a bit but would become moody when the caffeine left my body.

Things got so bad that I started getting headaches if I didn't have enough caffeine each day.

I can't remember the exact year, but in my mid-twenties, I stopped having caffeinated drinks.

My main drink each day is: A cup of green tea in the morning, water (or sparkling water), and some Lactaid-free milk.

After I changed what I put in my body, I noticed direct benefits. I wasn't as moody, and the middle-aged belly started to fade.

For eating, my doctor has recommended that I follow the Mediterranean diet.

This isn't your typical diet but a recommendation on the types of food to eat. Now I'm a firm believer in setting up healthy eating and drinking habits.

If you're struggling and currently have a high sugar and caffeine diet, talk to your doctor and see if she can offer some help. For me, the simple act of watching what I put into my body has made a big difference.

DAY 43: LOVE YOURSELF

I am hard on myself. I have always held myself up to an extremely high standard. My reasoning is pretty simple: As a kid, I didn't always have a stable upbringing, so I never knew when the rug would be pulled out from under me.

To deal with that, I fell back on making sure that I did everything I could to take care of myself and my immediate family.

I got great grades in school, worked hard, did my chores, and wasn't much of a troublemaker (though my brother and I used to clash a lot when we were kids).

I learned at an early age that I needed to work hard to get ahead, but I didn't take much time to love myself. I liked myself well enough, but I kept putting pressure on what I needed to achieve.

To be honest, I still do that. I push myself too hard.

A few weeks ago, my son was playing some music and I heard for the first time Dana Williams' song "Hard." It's basically a song about being too hard on yourself. The song hit home, and I stopped to look her song up on Spotify and played it.

I admit that I am also hard on myself, and that translates to how I expect others to live up to my own impossibly high standards.

Beneath all of this struggle, I work hard to love myself. I work to accept that I can't do everything all in one day and that making mistakes is okay.

Are you hard on yourself? Do you focus on everything but taking time for yourself?

I don't mean to say that you should be selfish. No.

I believe that we need to take care of our physical, emotional, psychological, and spiritual well-being.

Giving ourselves love is critical.

How to do that?

Simple. I like Gay Hendricks' recommendation in his book *Learning to Love Yourself*. The next time you are having a difficult time, stop and tell yourself that you love yourself for that. For example, if you're worried about losing your job, tell yourself that you love yourself that you're upset about that. Accepting and embracing the angst/fear/anger that you're feeling is a great way to ensure that you love yourself.

Try it, and over time it'll help.

DAY 44: HOW TO STOP WORRYING

I remember waiting for the bus back when I was in college, and I would start coughing when it pulled up. I had a nervous cough. When I'd get stressed out and worry, I'd start to cough and would feel like I had to get sick.

I'd worry about whether I'd do well in school, where I was going to get the money to pay off my college loans and a whole host of other things.

I'm a worrier.

I'm not happy about this and work hard to deal with this quirk of mine.

But when I look back at my childhood, I can understand where my worrying started. After my father left and my mom moved back into her parents' home with my younger brother and me, my default state was to worry.

I even tried to forecast what I needed to worry about and pre-think through possible situations. I liked to be prepared and never liked surprises.

(I understand why some people like surprise parties, but I don't.)

I had enough surprises in growing up, and they often weren't good ones.

Back when I was in elementary school, I remember going to church with my classmates. It was a special mass in which during the "Peace be with you" part, we were supposed to turn around and go out of our pews to meet up with our parents to shake their hand and offer them peace.

Unfortunately, no one showed up for me that day. My mom needed to work, and for some reason, not sure why to this day, neither of my grandparents could see me (both were retired).

I stood there in mass, and I began to worry. What would happen when everyone went to see their parents, and I would be left there alone. Who would I shake hands with? What was I going to do?

The big moment came, and the boys next to

me left the pew to go to see their parents. Everyone did the same thing, but me.

I stood there, and I felt as though the temperature in the church went from comfortable to "oh no, I feel sick, it's so hot." And that's what I did. I threw up all over the pew in front of me.

I felt shame, fear, and unloved.

I don't remember much after that. I don't know who helped clean me up or anything else. But the worry and shame remain with me to this day.

I am no stranger to worrying. I'm older now and have more tools at my fingertips to help deal with anxiety. I hope that one of these tips are a help to you.

Muscle relaxation

Before any stressful situation, I clench my fists up tight, take a slow intake of air, hold for several seconds, and then, as I exhale, I slowly unclench my fists.

If I have more privacy, then I'll work by doing my hands, then feet, clench my teeth, lift the tongue of my mouth to the roof of my mouth and then finally hold all my muscles clenched, hold the breath and then exhale slowly.

By taking control of my fear and worry, I focus on my body and that I'll be okay.

Your mind is more powerful than you think

When my brain is in worry mode, I'll get hit with all sorts of thoughts: What if x, y, or z doesn't happen? What if I don't have enough money? What if they don't like me? What if, what if, what if…

Playing into those negative thoughts only increases the problem. What I've learned to do is this:

I worry for a few minutes, then stop and think of something else. When my willpower is weak, I let my mind go back to worrying, but change my thoughts after only two minutes. In about 10 minutes, I've refocused my mind onto something positive.

That could be something as simple as saying repeatedly in my head: "I know I can, I know I can, I know I can." Or, if I'm stressed out, I'll add a bit of a spiritual twist to things: "Let go, let go." And if things are so bad that I'm really out of sorts, I'll say the serenity prayer: "God, grant me the serenity to accept the things I cannot change, the courage to change the things I can and wisdom to know the difference."

These tips are easy to do and have helped me time and time again.

Do I still worry? Yes, I do. Not as much as I used to as a young adult, but now I have the skills to help stop the worrying. I hope these tips help you. And if you've gone through the sorts of worrying as I have (with getting stressed and sick), I've been there. You're not alone.

DAY 45: OVERCOMING SHAME

What is that most shameful moment that you look back to as a kid that just stays with you?

For me, it's being a little kid sitting at the table having dinner. My father comes home from work, and he gets upset at what my mom has made. I remember him saying that he worked all day and came home to have a crappy meal.

I froze, and a bolt of fear shot through me.

My mom did not confront him, but my father's anger went from 0 to 60 in just a few seconds. He threw back the kitchen chair that went flying across the room and then stormed out.

I don't remember eating the rest of my dinner,

but I do remember going outside on my Big Wheel.

I felt shame that I didn't know what I could do to help my mom.

Of course, it's easy for me to tell myself now that there's nothing I could have done as a kid.

But in the moment, that's not what I felt. I drove my Big Wheel up the block. I heard kids playing across the street, but I just went up and down the block on my Big Wheel and listened as I crunched the fallen leaves underneath the wheels.

The kids across the street were laughing and having a good time, and I felt so lost, scared, and a deep sense of shame. There was something wrong with my family. And since I was part of the family, that meant that there was something wrong with me.

I didn't know what that was. I didn't know how to express it, but I could feel the shame in every atom of my body.

That is what shame does to you.

Bestselling author and shame researcher Brené Brown defines shame as: "the intensely painful feeling that we are unworthy of love and belonging."

Her advice is to reach out and to be brave. To

share our story and our shame with those we trust helps to lead us to the path of healing.

The rough times that I grew up with have helped set how I react in a crisis. And when I peel away all those feelings of my childhood, I expose the shame. Shame that I couldn't stop what happened in my family and to my mother, but also shame that I would grow up and be like my father.

That fear, mixed with anger, and shame is a poisonous concoction that tried to keep me down.

To overcome shame, I find these tools help:

- **Journaling.** When I write my feelings out, I can be sure that my emotions are released in a safe and respected space.
- **Talking.** I have talked with loved ones and therapists who have been kind enough to help guide me and listen to my stories.
- **Let go.** The stories of my past are a broken record that keeps skipping and tries to lock me in the past. It would be easy to allow my past stories to stop

me from growing. But if I were to allow that, then I would never grow.

Life is cyclical, and there are times when I am strong and times when I am weak. When I am weak, the old shame stories come back to haunt me. That is when I need to take the skills that I have learned and put them into practice.

If you're looking for help in overcoming shame, I recommend watching Brown's TED talk "Listening to Shame" and picking up a copy of her book *The Gifts of Imperfection: Let Go of Who You Think You're Supposed to Be and Embrace Who You Are*.

I have found both to be of great help.

DAY 46: TAKE A FEW STEPS FORWARD EACH DAY TOWARD YOUR GOAL

I have had some big dreams in my life. What are your dreams?

How are you going to achieve them?

If we take just a few steps forward each day, that work becomes the building block of our completed goal.

But it's hard to think this way.

We want the instant fix, the quick answer, and it's not easy to persevere and move forward toward our goal.

As a kid, my teachers kept telling us about the tortoise and the hare. The hare would run fast, get tired out, and lose the race.

We're not in a race with anyone but ourselves.

If you want to write a book, write a couple of hundred words a day. Want to run a 5K? Find a training plan and follow it.

Imagine what the builders of the great medieval Gothic cathedrals went through. The churches they built took hundreds of years to finish, but thousands of people completed the work.

Today you might take three steps forward and tomorrow four steps back, but the next day you might go five steps forward.

Keep moving forward.

If you fail, try again. If you fail another time, adapt, be flexible, try a different idea or another way.

When we allow ourselves to be stuck, we're agreeing to remain imprisoned in our situation. There's no need to look for others to save us. Be your own hero.

But by continuing to move forward, we're growing and will eventually achieve our goal.

One step at a time.

If you think about it, that's what we all do.

DAY 47: IT'S OKAY TO ASK FOR HELP

A few years back, I tried to move a big bookcase on my own. I needed to move it about a foot and thought that I could knock it out in a few minutes and be on my way.

I put my weight against the bookcase, struggled with it for a few minutes, and I succeeded.

However, later in the day, a dull backache from moving the bookcase flared up to be so painful that I could barely stand up straight.

It took me four days for me to feel better and the back pain to subside.

Looking back, it's easy for me to admit that I should have asked for help. But I didn't.

Why?

I grew up in an alcoholic and dysfunctional family. Sometimes I would get the help I needed when I asked for it, but other times, I didn't. That might have been because of any number of things. I learned quickly that if I wanted something done, then I needed to do it myself.

I took on more work and made certain that I accomplished what I put my mind to. Too often, I have been let down by those who were supposed to take care of me. There's no use crying over spilled milk, but I do believe it's important to admit how I feel and then see where I am today.

When I ask for help, I feel weak. Sometimes I'm ashamed to ask for help because I feel stupid or inferior. My hang-ups might be swirling around in my head, trying to convince me to be quiet and just go about my own business.

I'm used to working on my own. I set a goal, I accomplish it and go on my way.

The challenge is when we're up against a tough problem or task. We can't do everything on our own.

When I wanted to start my gaming podcast back in the early 2000s, I came up with the idea but didn't know where to start. I reached out to a podcast and asked for help.

What did he do? He put together some documentation to teach me what I needed to know and sent it to me to help.

Back in 2011, when I wanted to publish my first *Cinderella's Secret Diaries* book, I had no clue how to create the ebook file. I knew HTML and some basic coding but didn't know where to start. I did a Google search, found Guido Henkel, who wrote a blog on how to create an ebook, and emailed him for help.

What did he do? He responded to my questions and helped me out. Since then, I've referred other indie authors to him and recommended that they pick up his book.

Over the years, time and time again, people helped me when I asked.

So why do I have such a hard time asking for help?

I'm afraid.

When I overcome my fears, doors open to me, and good things happen that I couldn't have predicted.

I'm a big believer in passing it forward. Help is a two-way street. Today I might need help, tomorrow I can help another.

If I stop and think about the cyclical nature of

work and put the bigger picture into perspective, everyone needs help at some point in their lives. Maybe that's professional guidance about your career, counseling to overcome a problem, technical help with a phone or computer, or a whole list of other things. The beauty of accepting help is that you can help others at any time.

Give and take. Take and give.

The next time you're ready to push a heavy bookcase across the room and think you can do it alone, maybe it might be a good idea to stop and ask for help. Your back will thank you

DAY 48: YOU HAVE ALWAYS BEEN WHOLE

I am broken, different, wrong, and will never be whole.

Have you ever thought of any of that?

It's hard. I know.

I have often felt the odd person out as I do my best to fit in with the crowd. For many years, I tried to make up for my perceived shortcomings by throwing myself into my studies and then work.

I knew I was different by how I grew up, but I didn't know what to do about it.

As a teenager, I'd dream of meeting someone, fall in love, and that together with my half and hers we would meld into one complete spirit.

Kind of shows where my head was back in those days.

I never imagined that I was complete. I could not say the words:

"I have always been whole. I am enough."

Sit with that thought for a few moments.

How do those words make you feel?

Are you laughing because you feel that they're not true? Are you denigrating yourself because you see what a screwup you think you are? Your faults, quirks, the mistakes you've made all along the way?

Back in college I took a world religion course, and our professor taught us about Hinduism. Having grown up Catholic, I found Hinduism foreign but comforting. In one lesson, the professor taught us about that Atman (our soul) and the universal Brahman, which was the Absolute.

He ended his lesson by telling us that the Atman and Brahman were the same. We were creation. Creation was us.

I filed that away in the back of my brain but came back to it a few years ago when starting Deepak Chopra's 21-day meditation plan. Chopra talked about creation and how our uniqueness makes us complete.

Think of it this way: All of creation is whole. the galaxies, the stars, planets, even every atom is all part of creation. The sum of everything is whole and makes up our universe—from the largest black hole to the smallest sub-atomic particle; everything is part of creation. If the universe is whole and we're part of the universe, that makes us whole as well.

The trick here is that we allow ourselves to see ourselves as weak, damaged, or broken.

Imagine if we pulled the wool from over our eyes and empowered ourselves to see our true nature. Quirks, mistakes, and all. Wouldn't that be wonderful.

I have always been whole.

Say that out loud. Sit with that sentence for a moment and think about what it means for you. You might not believe it and can give a laundry list of problems that you have. But what if you turn the switch on within yourself to see outside the shame and fog that we all grew up with in an alcoholic/dysfunctional family?

What if we allowed ourselves to believe the truth?

We have always been whole. We only allow

ourselves to be trapped because it's what we grew up with and how we adapted to survive.

There's a choice here: We can choose to see ourselves as damaged, whole, or somewhere in-between.

Why not be free and try on the thought:

"I have always been whole."

Let that sit with you for a bit longer.

Write it down and put it down where you can see it every day.

It might take time to believe but it's the truth.

It's your truth.

DAY 49: NAME THREE GOOD THINGS IN YOUR LIFE

It's easy to be negative. Too easy.

Each day when you get up, take a moment to think of three good things in your life. What are they? Name them, say them, and own them.

The negativity spiral is enticing, and the slid from bad to worse happens fast.

I grew up in a dysfunctional/alcoholic family. To survive, I started thinking the worst possible outcome would happen, and I'd plan for how to avoid that as best I could. But the sad thing is that by always thinking the worst, I limited myself from joy and freedom.

Negativity saps joy.

But imagine when we see the positive in life and embrace it.

What are your three good things in your life?

I'm not saying that we avoid the pain, suffering, and difficulty we're going through. That's not how life is. The truth is that each day we have a mix of the good and the bad.

How we choose to deal with the negativity and go through life is another thing, though.

Malala Yousafzai of Pakistan was nearly killed when several men fired on her school bus back in 2012. The Taliban wanted her to suffer for keeping a diary about her life. Instead of giving up, she took her message of the importance of educating young women around the world and became the youngest Nobel Peace Prize winner at 17-years-old.

Having been shot in the head, she survived, recovered, and thrived.

I have been writing to the subscribers of my fantasy series for more than six years now and I've heard from some of my readers who have struggled with chronic diseases, loss of a spouse, cancer, or struggling to make ends meet after losing a job. Their stories of resilience and of positivity inspire me.

Every day we wake up and have a choice.
What are three good things are in your life? Name them.

Day 50: Your Life Is Precious and Beyond Compare

No matter how difficult your life and what you're going through, you are one-of-a-kind. You are amazing and beautiful. You are beyond compare.

Of course, that's easy to write and say, but do each of us believe it?

Probably not.

I know that I often deal with negative criticism within my head. That critical voice that tells me that I'm not good enough, I have so much to learn, and that I will always struggle.

Last week, I saw a tragic event. A man had collapsed on the train platform—the platform that I stand every day on the way to work. The police and medical personnel tried to revive him and then put him on a stretcher to get him to a hospital. As two other passengers and I spoke with a police officer, I asked him if they were able to revive the man. He shook his head and the thought sunk in: He had died.

Whatever family he had, they would eventually hear the news and would grieve him.

There was nothing that the medical team could do to bring him back, and they tried everything they could—four or five people worked to try to bring him back, but they failed.

We had been asked to stay so that we could give our statements to the police, and I felt helpless. The experts worked to try and save the man, and I stood off to the side waving my hands in the air to flag down additional police and a second ambulance crew that came on the scene.

That man's life was precious, as is yours.

None of us know how much time we have on this Earth, and maybe that's a good thing.

Today is your chance to take another step toward healing and joy.

If you can't do it on your own, then ask for help. If you're afraid, then overcome that fear.

The time we have now is all we got.

How are you going to use the time you have today?

DAY 50: YOUR LIFE IS PRECIOUS AND BEYOND COMPARE

No matter how difficult your life and what you're going through, you are one-of-a-kind. You are amazing and beautiful. You are beyond compare.

Of course, that's easy to write and say, but do each of us believe it?

Probably not.

I know that I often deal with negative criticism within my head. That critical voice that tells me that I'm not good enough, I have so much to learn, and that I will always struggle.

Last week, I saw a tragic event. A man had collapsed on the train platform—the platform that I stand every day on the way to work. The police and medical personnel tried to revive him and then put him on a stretcher to get him to a hospital. As two other passengers and I spoke with a police officer, I asked him if they were able to revive the man. He shook his head and the thought sunk in: He had died.

Whatever family he had, they would eventually hear the news and would grieve him.

There was nothing that the medical team could do to bring him back, and they tried everything they could—four or five people worked to try to bring him back, but they failed.

We had been asked to stay so that we could give our statements to the police, and I felt helpless. The experts worked to try and save the man, and I stood off to the side waving my hands in the air to flag down additional police and a second ambulance crew that came on the scene.

That man's life was precious, as is yours.

None of us know how much time we have on this Earth, and maybe that's a good thing.

Today is your chance to take another step toward healing and joy.

If you can't do it on your own, then ask for help. If you're afraid, then overcome that fear.

The time we have now is all we got.

How are you going to use the time you have today?

DAY 51: WHAT WOULD YOU SAY TO YOUR YOUNGER SELF

If I could go back and talk to my younger self, I would tell him to relax more and that all would turn out fine. I spent a lot of time and energy, worrying about the stupidest of things.

I worried about whether I could ever find someone who would love me, worried about dumb things that I had done, and even worried about whether I'd find happiness.

I think that's the tricky thing about growing up in an alcoholic/dysfunctional family—I always waited for something bad to happen. When you grow up with uncertainty, change, and your fear of it, you're wired that way.

In looking back, I wish I had someone who I

could have talked to, who would have shared with me some wisdom or advice on how to get through some of the difficult times. I didn't have that, and I can't go back to fix any of those times.

Using this exercise to pretend that I could go back in time is helpful because I can use that same advice today or for my future self.

I still struggle with worrying.

But being more mindful of my struggles and the challenges I go through is helpful.

What works for me might not work for you.

Write a letter to your younger self and see what you put down in it. Good luck and be easy on yourself.

DAY 52: THE POWER OF JOURNALING

Somewhere in my attic I still have my daily journals that I wrote back when I was 16-years old. The angst, fear and worries that I struggled with are captured on dot matrix printed paper from when I used to own a Commodore 64 computer.

I would sit at the computer late at night, put my fingers to the keyboard and just write. I think I have more than 500 pages of those early journals still.

What I learned during my teen years was this simple fact:

Writing helped me.

If I could think thoughts and put those thoughts down on paper, then I had a way of reconciling my feelings with how I acted and behaved. I could use journal writing to exorcise my inner demons.

I wrote about my family, my first girlfriend and how lost and alone I felt in the world.

The power that I gained through writing gave me hope.

By writing, I could put down my thoughts about anything. There was no topic that was out-of-bounds. Better yet, I could write anything I wanted and feel physically better after my writing session.

And when I needed that extra bit of help, I had two special tricks up my sleeve:

- Write with my fingers on the keys but with my eyes closed.
- Allow myself the freedom to write whatever I wanted, but I didn't save the journal entry.

Both means of journal writing boosted my self-confidence, strengthened my self-esteem, and helped me heal from my problems.

I could write out possible solutions, try out ideas, have conversations with people—I had the freedom to write whatever I wanted, and that built out trust within me.

I quickly realized that I could overcome my problems by writing about them, coming up with solutions, and coming to terms with my feelings.

Back in the '80s, there wasn't a way for a teen to go to counseling. Sure, it happened, but in my family, asking for something like that would not have been possible. I didn't get to therapy until I had my own health insurance.

As a teen, writing in my journal gave me the help I needed to ground me.

Let Your Fingers Go

If you've never tried journal writing, start small. First, decide on whether you want a physical journal to write in or a digital one (Google doc, Word file, Evernote, etc.).

Then simply make time to do the writing. Start slow and easy.

1. Pick a time of day that you want to write and stick with it (before work or bed might be best as those times become part of your routine.)
2. In the beginning, set the length of time that you want to write. Maybe 5-10 minutes might work best in the beginning. I like to write, so I can go on for a bit as I like getting into a flow state.
3. When writers' block comes, keep writing. Even if you need to talk about the weather or repeat a sentence over and over again, keep at it. Some questions to help:

- How do you feel as you're writing?
- What happened to you that day?
- What are you doing tomorrow?
- Give yourself the freedom to write. This is the tricky part. In the beginning, you might fear that

someone will find your journal. Depending on whether you have a physical journal or a digital one, make time to protect it. The journal is for you. Not your spouse or really anyone else.
- Let go and just be when you write.
- When you do start writing, over time, it'll become easier as you become used to the practice. I'd recommend sticking with it for two weeks. If you like it after that, keep writing. If not, move on and try something else.

For me, writing and creativity have helped save me. I don't know who I would be today without them!

DAY 53: STOP BLAMING OTHERS FOR YOUR PROBLEMS

It's easy to get caught up in the maelstrom of our upbringing. For a long time, I blamed my father for how difficult things were in my life. He left my mom, he didn't pay child support, and he didn't take the time to be a positive role model for me.

But that's not entirely true. At least for the first five years of my life, he did work and paid for the house, clothes, and food that we ate. And he wasn't always a bad person. No one ever is. I remember being sick as a little kid, and my father took me in his arms. He held me up and said, "Just let your stuffed-up nose go into me. I'll take your sickness from you."

There were other people around, and the

thought that my father wanted to help me sent a positive ripple through me. He did care.

As I got older, I reflected on my childhood, I always thought back to the bad stuff. The fights, the yelling, and his not being there. He checked out, moved on, and remarried (and had more kids).

My brother and me became the afterthought. We didn't matter anymore.

I held that anger and disappointment in me like a weapon.

It was his fault that my mom, brother, and I suffered as much as we did.

It's easy to see someone as the bad guy. What's more difficult is to see the complexities of a situation and the larger context of what happened to my father. He went to Vietnam and fought in the war, was wounded, and I expect he dealt with PTSD. But no one really ever talked about any of that back in the early '70s.

My father's story and how we reacted to it set into motion his life and affected all our lives. This is true.

However, when I became older and went to college, I learned about how the trauma that my mom went through had affected my brother and me. At that point, I had a choice: I could continue to blame my father for my problems, or I could work to find healing and learn better behaviors.

I learned what I experienced. I allowed the effects of alcoholism and the dysfunction to set me on a course that had me constantly fearing abandonment, authority, and true connection. I acted out of fear, anger, and shame. By pointing a finger at my father, I didn't accept responsibility for myself and my own actions.

When I changed that and worked toward bettering myself, the world shifted.

I couldn't use my father as a scapegoat any longer. I had to grow up and face the facts: If I wanted to change, then I needed to mature.

I have made (and will continue to make) lots of mistakes in my life.

But there's a difference now—I own up to making the mistake and work each day toward becoming a better person.

When I hurt someone, I don't blame my father for how I acted. No, I admit my mistake and work on fixing the problem.

I am responsible.

The shift in power is eye-opening.

What do you think will happen if you stop

blaming others or making excuses for where you are?

I do not mean berating yourself. That is not my point. But if you want to get from a place of hurt to one of freedom and wholeness, only you have the power to do that.

Exhilarating and frightening all at the same time.

Today I choose to stop blaming and own up to my faults. If I can do this, so can you.

DAY 54: GIVE YOURSELF PERMISSION TO BE HAPPY

As the oldest child who grew up in an alcoholic/dysfunctional family, I took on a lot of responsibility. I took on the emotional burden of the problems my mother suffered through and needed to find a way to make a path for myself. I threw myself into school, work, and creativity.

I survived by using my imagination to dream up new worlds, creatures, and places.

But I worked hard and always felt that the rug would be pulled out from under me at any time. I lived life as though an earthquake could raze everything that I had built in my life.

Happiness seemed an elusive and temporary moment for me. Terrence Malick's film *To the*

Wonder with Ben Affleck in it comes to mind. Olga Kurylenko is Affleck's love interest in the film. She goes through an extremely difficult time in the movie but has these flashes of brilliance. There's a scene in which she's running through the fields, stops, and turns back. A bright light shines directly on her face and illuminates her like she's seen an angel of God.

Watching that scene reminds me of how I grew up and how I also used to think about creativity. I would have brief flashes of happiness that would be snatched away from me. And when I did write and create things, I used to wait "for the muse" to inspire me. I'd write stories and books when I felt inspired.

When I look back, I can now compare how I wrote with exercise: I can't imagine running a marathon without putting in the training. I've run three marathons, and it takes months of training, and that's after you have a solid core base of running (normally, running experts recommend having two years of running under your belt). There is no way I could run one day, then pick it up two weeks later, and then run for two days straight and suddenly think I could run a marathon. I'd hurt myself if I had tried that.

Being creative, it's the same thing. I need to put in the work each day. I write on a schedule and have learned that writing makes me happy.

I have given myself permission to embrace life and feel better. Part of that means that I exercise regularly and do the same with writing.

But for a long time, I didn't permit myself to be happy. I'd chase happiness, be ecstatic for a while, and then my world would fall apart. I'd find a woman I had a crush on, fall in love with being in love, chase after that fleeting dream, and all would crash to the ground. I'd be unhappy, upset, hurt, and the cycle would start over again after a time.

A lot changed in my life after I realized that I could be happy on my own. I could find strength in myself and joy in who I am—and stopped trying to define myself through the love of another.

When you permit yourself to be happy, doors will open for you in ways that you cannot comprehend.

How to start?

Take a small first step.

You can do it.

DAY 55: BE THE CHANGE YOU WANT IN THE WORLD

How many times have you heard the phrase "Be the change that you want in the world" or something similar to that? You might think that the words are empty or sound trite.

What does it mean to "be the change"? What change? How? When?

When you feel broken and a victim of your circumstances, you will not be able to rise. Owning self-power and believing in your abilities takes effort.

I have heard time and time again how people want to be successful, rich, powerful, happy—whatever. But when I ask them: "How are you going to do that?' The responses I receive are pretty much all the same: "That's too hard." Or: "That person got lucky." There's always an excuse.

The only way I know of having sustained success in achieving your goals is by getting in the sandbox and working. We cannot build a masterpiece until we try and fail.

A great change takes effort. And effort means sustained energy over time.

When little, my grandfather taught me how to ride a bike. I was scared. He held the back of my seat, and I peddled, but I didn't have the strength, and I would fall. My grandfather stayed with me, and we kept trying and trying until I got it. Then I went out on my own and tried.

But the story goes on from there. Yes, I learned how to ride a bike, and like many kids in the '80s, I jumped ramps, went into the woods and jumped over all sorts of things. One day my friends and I had the "brilliant" idea of riding our bikes full speed around the local baseball diamond and then jam our brakes on as we came over home plate so that we could throw dirt (from braking fast) up in the air. Yeah, that would be cool. My one friend did it, another one did, and then I went.

I peddled as hard as I could, went around the bases, and stood up on my bike and peddled as fast as I could toward home plate. I went to break and turn the bike sideways so that the dirt would fly up in the air, but my brakes jammed. I didn't stop. I crashed right into the cage behind where the batter would stand and hurt myself.

After a hospital visit, along with several stitches, I learned a thing or two.

Did I give up bike riding? No. Did I stop being a fool running full speed at home plate to brake and look cool? Yes.

"Be the change you want in the world."

That's going to take time, effort, and practice, just like riding a bike.

The beauty of change and making a difference in the world is that you can do it right now. How? You're reading this, aren't you?

Now, what are you going to do after reading this post? What dream do you have that will help others and change the world for the better?

Change can be life-altering not only for making you money or physical items, but you can grow as a person and help others. It all depends on what you want.

The journey starts today and will end when your days on this earth come to pass.

When you try and take that first step, keep going. Fall, dust yourself off and get up.

Change takes time (and patience).

What are you waiting for?

DAY 56: GET UNSTUCK IN YOUR LIFE

If you feel stuck, or worse, going round and round in a circle, I hear you. I've been there.

One night before my Junior year in college started, I went outside near 2 a.m. and looked up at the sky. I lived with my grandparents, mom, and brother in a small row home. The summer heat had started to fade, but it was still warm enough to be outside in shorts. I stared up at the sky and watched the clouds pass by the moon.

And I wondered: What would the next year be like? Would I find love? What would I be when I "grew up"?

I had all these questions, but no answers.

Over the years, I have had many nights like

that. Typically, they take place in the fall, as I reflect on the past year.

I went through a lot of difficult times as a kid, and I wore that as a badge of shame. We never really talked about my father and what he did to my mom. And I grew up lost, confused, and hurt.

I have felt stuck in my life. I have felt doubt, fear, and resentment. I have also felt lost and unloved.

The only way I knew how to get out of those moments was to move onward.

For me, that meant writing. I wrote stories upon stories as a kid but then gave up writing when I became an adult. Deep down, I knew that writing could help heal me from the bad times of my childhood. And I also knew that my stories would give hope to others. But I stayed stuck.

In my early 20s, I looked up at the sky and wondered what I would do and be. Today, near 50, I still do the same thing. The difference is that I am willing to experiment, to try, and to fail.

If you want to heal, move on, and grow, then take the first step. Yes, it's scary, confusing, and there are no assurances. It doesn't matter if this is about a relationship, a job, going to a therapist, starting your own business, or facing an overwhelming personal problem.

There is a path before you. Might be left, right, backward, up, or down, who knows?

The only way I know to find solace and healing is to get my hands dirty and do the work. A book doesn't write itself. A job doesn't fall from on high into your lap. A relationship doesn't right itself. It takes work. Sometimes trial and error.

I found that those of us who grew up in alcoholic and dysfunctional homes tend to have a really hard time with change. It's easier to deal with the crap that we know than to try something new.

I want to share something with you. Last night I went to see *The Band's Visit*. The musical is about an Egyptian band who gets lost in Israel. They land in a small town and interact with the townsfolk who struggle with their day to day lives and feel stuck.

The song "Answer Me" is toward the end of the musical. A young man starts singing about his girlfriend as he hopes she'll call. And then the rest of the townsfolk sing about their hopes and dreams.

I invite you to listen to the song all the way to the end. When I hear the ending (I don't want to ruin it for you), tears well up in my eyes. Millions of people are searching for a better tomorrow. They look up to the sky and wonder what tomorrow will bring and how their lives will be better.

The answer will be different for each of us, but I believe it takes a straightforward action to begin.

Are you willing to become unstuck?

If so, then go onward and the rest you'll figure out along the way.

DAY 57: DEALING WITH DOUBT

Who am I to think that I could succeed?

I feel like a failure and am afraid. Or maybe I'm just delusional, and the dreams that I have are just fantasies.

I want to write books, create podcasts, teach through webinars, and share what I have to the world.

You're an impostor. Anything that you've tried to do, you fail, or at best, are mediocre. You'll never amount to anything.

I hear these thoughts in my head. It's not all the time, but when I'm tired, frightened, and worried, doubt creeps in and tries to convince me to give up on my dreams.

When my kids come to me and talk about their fears about failing in school or other parts of their life, I share my fears with them. I want them to know that adults doubt too. I have fears, and I worry.

I tell my kids stories about how I failed at work, but then I also tell them what I did to get past the problem, how I solved it and moved on. Not all problems have easy solutions, but I believe that there is a way to overcome doubt.

I have written eleven fiction books and two non-fiction ones so far. My dream is to write dozens more.

You suck as a writer. Remember that one-star review you got? You're wasting your time.

If I listened to the doubt and fear within me, then I would never be where I am today.

I believe that by owning our doubts and fears, sharing them with the world, we become free.

Sure, I might fail at work, with a book, or whatever. I fail at things more times than I can count.

But I get back up. I keep trying. I learn new things. I don't listen to my doubts and fears.

I think the most important lesson I've learned in life is to keep striving toward your goal. For me, that means writing and creating art. The dream has evolved over the years as technology has advanced so that now I create ebooks, print on demand books, I've done podcasts and built websites. My creativity is only limited by my imagination.

You'll never be successful. You suck. You should just shut up and give up and know your place.

When you have such negative thoughts, here's a trick to help you: Listen to your thoughts and then **embrace them. Tell yourself that you love that part of yourself.**

Try it, and you'll see. By giving that weak part of you love, you're accepting all parts of yourself.

Embrace the doubt and fear, share them with a trusted friend, love that part of yourself, and then let it go. Move on and keep reaching for your goal.

One step at a time.

DAY 58: TAKE A RISK

For a long time, I chose to stay quiet, keep to myself, and stay under the radar. I didn't want to rock the boat. I'm afraid of big changes. I like it when life is safe, secure, and calm. On the one hand, having stability can be a good thing, but on the other, without change, we cannot grow.

What is one thing that you could do to take a risk?

Some people are adrenaline junkies, and risk is their second name. That's not what I'm talking about.

A long time ago, I wanted to read some of my poems at a poetry reading at the now-defunct Borders. I asked all my friends if they could support me because I was afraid, but none of them could make it.

I then had to decide: Go on my own or stay home.

I thought about it over the week and decided that if I wanted to be a writer, then I needed to show up. That night I went to the reading, read my poems, and hand a good time.

But it was what happened to me afterward that changed my life.

I stayed late to help a friend put some folding chairs away when out of nowhere, a young woman came up to my friend. They talked for a bit, I was introduced to her, and we agreed to go out Valentine's Day.

That's how I met my wife.

You never know what might come your way. Over the years, when I'm asked to speak at an event or take part in something a bit outside my comfort zone, I weigh the option, and if the situation is good for me, then I take the risk.

Is it hard sometimes to do that? Yes, it is.

But I realize that growth means challenging myself.

When a friend asked me to help serve food to the homeless, I said yes. When my work asked that we make peanut butter and jelly sandwiches for a local food bank, I said yes. And when I was afraid to read my poems to strangers, I took the risk, and a door opened to me that I had not thought possible.

I know it's scary. I know that not every risk will mean sunrise and rainbows.

But sometimes saying yes can put you on a path of such grace and beauty that your life will be changed forever for the better.

And all it takes is to be open to change.

DAY 59: TAKING THE FIRST STEP TOWARD HEALING

I have been trapped into "all or nothing" thinking. I think that's because of the extremes that I went through as a kid. I often felt trapped in a situation that I couldn't get out of and would get frustrated with my supposed lack of power.

I suspect that my mother felt the same way.

What I didn't understand is that I did have power and that to break out of a mental prison, I needed to think differently.

I became the first person in my family to go to college and I attribute education as my ticket to freedom. By learning about the world, others different than me, and being put in contact with sociology and psychology classes, I learned that I had a choice. I could break free of my self-limiting thinking.

Before, I used my imagination to escape. I created fantasy worlds and wrote a book and lots of short stories. I found a way to take my pain and make art out of it.

Being creative helped me find a way to deal with my emotions and feelings, but I still needed to learn a path on how to model healthier behavior. What do I mean by that?

I realized that my relationships often suffered because I had an unhealthy history of what I thought love should be. Once I went to college and learned about the effects of alcoholism and how dysfunctional behaviors affected people, I stumbled upon the Adult Children of Alcoholics' laundry list.

Once I realized that I had taken on some of the characteristics of an alcoholic, that opened my eyes. Did it hurt to admit to myself that I had such characteristics? Yes.

I realized that I had stayed in some unhealthy relationships because I was afraid of abandonment. And I had chosen girls to date because I thought I could "fix them." I wanted to help another but was blind to my faults.

If you have similar traits to the ones listed on the ACA laundry list, I recommend that you do one thing first. Take a step back, list the characteristics that you have, and then love those parts of yourself. Trying to ignore, hide, or excise the faults you have will only make things worse.

The first step toward healing is to embrace your pain, accept it, and then let it go.

What I've learned is that acceptance and then loving yourself, helps you to let go of the fear and hurt (and often shame) around personality traits that have held you back.

When I let go of beating myself up for how I am, I can then take steps to help myself. What I have had to do is retrain my brain and how I act. To do that, I have gone to counseling over the years, attended Adult Children of Alcoholics Anonymous meetings, read books, added meditation, and exercise into my life, and decided to change my life.

The beautiful thing, though it's hard to see, is that I compare working on myself as a hike through the woods. When I come across a fork in the road, I have a choice. I can choose behaviors, people, and activities that will help me become a better person. And when I stumble, I can get back up again.

I see life as a journey. I don't know how long my road will go, but the beauty of life is that each day is a new beginning. Instead of feeling trapped in a lousy relationship, friendship, job, whatever, we have a choice we can make each day. Even if the step is just a small one in a direction that will help us, small changes turn into bigger ones over time.

The first step toward healing is a simple thought.

"I accept who I am. I love myself. And I want to grow and heal."

How?

Well, that's for each person to figure out though there are tools and activities to help us.

Why not try something and see what works for you?

DAY 60: HOW YOU FEEL ABOUT CHANGE IF YOU GREW UP IN AN ALCOHOLIC/DYSFUNCTIONAL FAMILY

By the time I entered 8th grade, I had attended a total of four schools. As a kid, I'd make friends but had to leave them behind to go to a new school. Add on top of that my insecurities of being skinny and someone who liked books; I found it difficult to deal with change in growing up.

When I look back at my childhood, I have memories that stand out and are painful.

The basic things that a lot of my friends grew up with (stability and secure in their home) weren't always in my family.

The complicated part of having grown up in an alcoholic/dysfunctional family is that you don't know any better. You grow up thinking that your life is "normal" and just like everyone else's.

Now as an adult, there are some things that I really dislike:

- Surprises
- Changes

Let me be clear: I don't mind making the changes, but I sure as hell don't like to be affected by other people's changes that come out of the blue.

When unplanned changes come up, I remember my childhood, and that increases my anxiety, and fear takes over (sometimes panic).

Here's how things typically go:

Out of the blue change, fear, anxiety, stress and sometimes anger.

Being the oldest kid in my family, I took on the super responsibility role. I'd be told as a kid: "You're the man of the house now and need to watch out for your mom." And I did do that, as best I could.

Now, as an adult, I have that over-responsible

gene burned into me, and when change comes, I have difficulty accepting it. I'm the planner, the organizer and like to be one step ahead. Unplanned changes throw me off my game.

But having difficulty accepting change is a common personality trait in children who grew up in alcoholic/dysfunctional households.

Have you ever felt this way?

Well, it seems that we're in good company.

The pressure to deal with change can be difficult to process and handle when my emotions are all over the place.

What do I do when I feel this way?

I think the most important thing is to recognize what I'm feeling. That might seem pretty straightforward, but in the moment, even just saying: "I'm feeling this way because of my childhood" helps.

Then I need some time to process how I'm feeling and come back to the table to talk it out.

There's great power in admitting that I'm reacting to a situation because of my upbringing. Owning how I feel and accepting it allows me to take the next step and move on.

The next step is to ask: "Is it true?"

Is it true that this is the end of the world? Is it

true that whatever I'm afraid of is going to ruin me?

Probably not.

The biggest challenge for me is separating my fears that spring up from my childhood and what's relevant today. How easy it is for the negative thoughts to spring up and play over and over in my head.

Breaking that cycle and challenging how I'm feeling can be difficult to do if I'm tired or feeling insecure.

And if there's a level of trust in the event (the players involved in the change aren't reliable, etc.), then that only adds more complexity to the problem.

But all isn't lost.

What I've learned over time is that most change is usually predictable. Granted, there are some changes that spring up unexpectedly, but as an adult, being nimble and flexible in the moment can be a Godsend.

To get to that more comfortable space, I've done a lot of work over the years. The top three things I'd recommend would be:

1. Write in a journal or talk to a trusted friend (or therapist) about how you feel.
2. Go for a walk or run. Get the body moving and allow yourself the time to think while you exercise. Just let yourself be.
3. Meditate. Give yourself the space you need to distance from the change. Build up the self-confidence by using meditation to re-center yourself.

The challenge, of course, is putting these skills into practice. Just like anything else in life, you need to put in the work to have them help you.

If you have a partner and are going through a difficult time in accepting change, be honest with them. Let them know how you feel and ask for some space/time to process what you're going through. And then, come back to them and talk things out.

The bigger challenge is that in the workplace, you might not have the luxury of having a safe psychological environment. Layoffs happen, firings, and reorganizations. Roll with the punches, but the tricky aspect of such change in the workplace is that your emotions might bleed out in your private life (having a shorter temper with your family as you struggle with the change). Be mindful of this.

Again, this is where honesty and putting your skills into practice will help.

Building a safety net today will help you tomorrow.

Is this easy? No, sometimes it isn't. I've been hurt, upset, stressed out, and dealing with anxiety when big unexpected change comes.

Knowing how to handle the change, will put you not only in a better frame of mind but set you up to be more flexible in handling change.

Growing up in an alcoholic/dysfunctional family does not mean that you have to be defined by what your life was like back then. Admitting what your struggles are and working on them, will help you be better prepared for when change comes. Again, sometimes things just suck and are difficult. That's life.

Yet how you respond to the change doesn't always have to be through stressing and freaking out.

DAY 61: BE ORIGINAL

We are all special in this world. We have unique fingerprints, and each of us can make or create whatever we can dream up.

I like to write, but I had a teacher after teacher (and family members) try to dissuade me from becoming an author. Why? People told me that it didn't pay a lot of money.

Still, I love to write, and I decided to keep writing (though I did have a big slump from my mid-20s up through my 30s). I wrote short stories, articles, essays, but I had given up on writing other books because I couldn't figure out how to get the book published.

Then the Kindle arrived, and indie publishing

exploded. That allowed me to use my creativity and dream up new worlds.

What do you want to do? How can you be original?

Are you an artist, a singer? Write music or recycle plastic bottles into unique art installations. Dream something up and make it.

For a long time, I let other people's opinions keep me in check. You don't have to do that. You can be original.

Like to write? Create a blog. Enjoy talking? Start a podcast.

If you need help with writing, there are many free author tools to help you (i.e., Google suite, Pocket, and Calibre).

And if inspiration is something that you need, I recommend that you watch Amanda Palmer's TED talk on The Art of Asking.

When I feel down, and people are trying to hold me back, I find the best medicine is to focus on the positive. Watching Amanda Palmer's video gave me a lot of inspiration and impressed me with her creativity and boldness.

And if you are still looking for some help on how to be original, then be sure to pick up Adam Grant's book *Originals: How Non-Conformists*

Move the World. We have so many opportunities to learn and to experiment with our creativity these days that there is plenty of room for us to explore and embrace art.

When I felt down and trapped as a kid, I created things. I wrote up stories, made up new worlds, and dreamed big.

Often as adults, we forget that we used to have that power. Find what used to make you happy as a kid and follow your passion.

I hope you enjoy the road ahead and embrace your creative side.

DAY 62: SETTING BOUNDARIES

I give, and I give, and I give and then usually blow up in frustration and need to pull back. I have always been the listener, the diplomat, the peacemaker.

But if I don't take care of myself, then I'm not useful to anyone.

I like to work behind the scenes, get the job done, do the planning, parse out the tasks, and then make my dream become a reality. I think that's why I enjoy writing books so much. I can take the work at my pace and know my strengths and weaknesses.

In my family life, I had to take on extra responsibility and started relying on myself at an early age. I accepted the responsibility because I understood that I needed to help out. Work and chores had to get done.

When I went to college, I started working with different people on class projects, and I hated that. I couldn't believe how unreliable some people were. They didn't do the work and felt that they were owed to have others cover for them (or they wanted to take credit for my work).

I didn't have time for that, and so I did the project, took care of myself, and went my way.

A friend of mine once said to me: "That's not your dog."

At first, I didn't understand what she meant, but she talked about a problem we had at work and pointed out that the issue wasn't my responsibility to fix. Her setting a clear boundary about what she needed to focus on and what she didn't made sense to me.

I just had never really put setting boundaries into active practice. Normally, I'd go along and be nice and then, like getting stung by a bee, I'd recoil back when I got stung.

Instead, I began setting up my boundaries at work, friendships, and in my family.

I am, by nature an introvert. Now that doesn't

mean that I'm shy. No, not at all. When I talk in front of a large group of people, I feel drained and not energized. Extroverts get charged up in talking to people. As an introvert, I become tired and need time alone to recharge.

By setting boundaries up, I can take care of myself from the get-go. That's important because if I listen and care too much, I'm not saving any energy and peace for myself.

Over the years I have come across people who talked about their problems constantly. They didn't want to solve their problems but liked talking about them. They talked just to talk. By setting boundaries, I found a natural and more balanced way to listen (to a point), and then disengage to focus on something else.

Boundaries are important because as you change and grow, the people in your life will take notice.

Sometimes that can be a challenge because friends and family don't want you to change. They might like using you as a person who will always care. When you pull back, don't be surprised if there's some backlash there. What I noticed is that when changes take place, my true friends will understand and accept that I need space.

If you grew up in an alcoholic or dysfunctional family, it's not uncommon that you're a people pleaser. You don't want to see conflict in a situation and want everyone to get along. Unfortunately, not everyone wants to play fair.

Some people want more of your time and energy because they know that they can take advantage of you.

If you set your boundaries early, then you can be extremely clear on where you stand.

A long time ago a person in my life used to try to guilt me into going along on things and meeting up, talking on the phone, and going places. I started to go along to be nice, but after a while, I set my boundaries and took some space. The friend didn't like this and tried to ratchet up the guilt, but I stayed strong. I took some flak from my friend because they wanted me to play a certain role in their life. But I didn't want that.

I made it clear that I would be friendly but that I needed to do my own thing and take care of myself.

The friend eventually pulled away because they couldn't get out of me what they wanted. I stood strong.

This same type of experience in boundary-setting has happened to me not just with friends but also at work. If you're aware of how to set boundaries, then you'll be better prepared.

Step one is pretty clear: What do you want to do?

Once you know what that is, then take steps to get to that point of calm. It won't be easy with some people, but your true friends will accept you for taking the space you need. And if this happens on the job, sometimes it's important to say no because it sets a precedent on how far you're willing to go (and lets people see that you're not a pushover).

DAY 63: LEARN TO LET GO

I work hard to solve problems, be better, and to grow.

But I learned that sometimes it's crucial to stop struggling and learn to let go.

That might seem counter-intuitive to you.

If something is beyond my control, I can spin, spin, and spin around trying to solve and fix the issue, but often, the problem is not mine to solve.

If you grew up in an alcoholic or dysfunctional home, you probably have taken on traits that create a self-fulfilling prophecy for yourself. For me, I have often poured lots of time and energy into people who could not be there for me emotionally. Another thing I have done over the years is to listen to someone's problems, thinking that they needed a sounding board so that they could solve their problems, but they only wanted to talk about themselves and not change.

I learned this lesson the hard way when I first started dating. I listened to a girlfriend to complain about her family for hours upon hours. She told me that she had decided to make a big change after we talked for eight hours on the phone. When I saw her a few days later, she had decided not to go down the path she had expressed with me. I realized then that she had only been looking for someone to complain to, and she didn't want to change and solve her problem.

The amount of energy and time I have wasted over the years in crossing boundaries and allowing myself to be dragged into the emotional mud of someone else's problem is considerable.

I learned how to put up strong boundaries but also to let go.

Instead of struggling and fighting against something that I could not change or solve, I found that stepping back and letting things go helped to solve the problem.

Some tips that I've used along the way to help me is to ask myself:

- Is this really my problem?
- Do I need to set a boundary with a person or a group of people?
- Is someone trying to use me to their advantage?

I like to help and solve problems. But sometimes it's important that I take a step back and take care of myself.

What situations are you in where taking a step back and letting go would help?

DAY 64: ONE STEP AT A TIME

For me, New Year's is long gone, and I expect that a lot of people's resolve on holding up to their resolutions has also been forgotten by now. We have the greatest of intentions, but then we give up on our promises.

Why is that?

When I watch TV and see the various diet plans during commercials, I find my answer. Pictures of slim men and women promise how they lost so many pounds and feel great. Often these diet plans come with purchasing special food. The thin actors smile and talk about how easy it is just to eat while losing weight.

And then I ask out loud: "What happens when you stop buying the special meals?"

People put the weight back on.

We cannot live our lives always on a diet. It's not how our brain works.

But we can take small steps each day to help orient us in the right direction. I read a book recently that mentioned a man who wanted to go to the gym and exercise. He had promised himself that he would lose weight but didn't know how to begin. So, for two weeks straight, he drove 20 minutes to the gym, stayed there and exercised for 5 minutes, and then came home.

Might sound odd, but he had a method to why he did that.

He knew that if he made an effort for two weeks straight to ingrain the habit of going to the gym and eased into it, that he would more readily accept the change in his life. His plan worked and he gradually increased his time in the gym.

We can take that same idea and apply it to our lives.

Small changes, over time, can lead to significant changes.

A few years back I read Charles Duhigg's *The*

Power of Habit: Why We Do What We Do in Life and Business, and that got me thinking about why I have certain habits and how to change the ones that aren't good for me (my weakness is late-night snacking right before bed).

My first therapist told me many moons ago that our habits fall into patterns like the grooves on a vinyl album. We need to retrain our brains to make new habits, and it takes time to do that. When we're in a stressful situation, our fall back habit might be to act a certain way. But we don't always have to respond like that. We can train ourselves to act differently.

Knowledge is power. It might sound like a corny quote, but I ascribe to that belief.

The more we know about ourselves, how our brain works, and who we are, the more we can take small steps to make big changes in our lives.

The first step: Knowledge.

Observe what your habits are: How you interact with people, what your quirks are, and decide what you'd like to change.

Instead of jumping right in, read about habits. Duhigg's book is a good start.

Taking control of our lives and starting out on

a new path is exhilarating though it can be frightening too.

The beauty of it all is that we only need to take one step at a time.

DAY 65: COMPASSION TOWARD OTHERS (AND YOURSELF)

If you turn on the news, or just stick your head outside a window, you'll see and hear the great hate debate that's raging across the world. Red vs. Blue. Black vs. White. The list goes on and on and on.

Compassion is not a popular word these days. It seems that people are either on the "right" or "wrong" side.

But I would disagree. To take a phrase from the bible, no person is "without sin."

I have done bad things. I have done things that are good. I am human. The problem these days is that we act as though everyone needs to be as perfect as they can be.

That's just not true.

In major cities across the U.S., hundreds of murders take place each year. There is a rise in hate crimes. My government has put migrant children in cages, and several of those children have died from the flu.

I don't know if it's because of my upbringing or my personality type (Myers-Briggs: INFJ) but I like to take a step back and see the bigger picture. Maybe it's because I'm a fantasy and science fiction writer but I think of things this way: We all live on the same planet. If an asteroid hit us, or a horrible disease breaks out, we're all going to die. Doesn't matter what side we are on.

We're all on the same planet. Astronomer Carl Sagan coined the term "pale blue dot" when scientists turned one of the Voyager spacecraft back at Earth and caught our tiny planet in a beam of sunlight. Sagan's pale blue dot speech became famous and has lived on nearly 30 years after his death.

He wrote:

"Look again at that dot. That's here. That's home. That's us. On it everyone you love, everyone you know, everyone you ever heard of, every human being who ever was, lived out their lives. The aggregate of our joy and suffering, thousands of confident religions, ideologies, and economic doctrines, every hunter and forager, every hero and coward, every creator and destroyer of civilization, every king and peasant, every young couple in love, every mother and father, hopeful child, inventor and explorer, every teacher of morals, every corrupt politician, every 'superstar,' every 'supreme leader,' every saint and sinner in the history of our species lived there-on a mote of dust suspended in a sunbeam."

Yet still, each day we kill, rape, and steal from each other all over the world. The complexities of why people cause harm to others are not as simple to understand. But violence typically comes due to power imbalance or in defense. Someone has more than others, feels oppressed, and lashes out. Or someone has power, exercises it on the powerless, and presses down.

Each of us has a decision to make each day. If you grew up in an alcoholic or dysfunctional home, you might have experienced violence firsthand. When under stress, your natural reaction might be to hit back (physically or emotionally).

Choosing compassion is not easy. Even my saying to be compassionate toward others might be too radical of a thought. (If your enemy is hurting you, turning the other cheek might seem saint-like and nearly impossible.)

But what if you take a simple step and practice compassion toward yourself?

A year ago, I took part in training and learned about the Loving-Kindness Meditation.

There are three parts to this meditation:

1. Send compassion, health, and peace toward yourself.
2. Send compassion, health, and peace toward a neutral person/enemy.
3. Send compassion, health, and peace out toward the world

For today, try saying these phrases five times to yourself each day:

May I be happy
May I be healthy
May I be peaceful

> May I live with ease

It only takes a minute or two, but you're setting the intention to focus on compassion toward yourself. Small steps get you to your destination.

I wish you the best in taking that first step.

DAY 66: FINDING SECURITY

I remember a night when my mom and stepfather had a big argument. I don't know what it was about because my brother and I were in our room getting ready for bed.

My mom came into our room and gave my brother and me a big hug. She started talking about leaving if that would make things better for all of us, and I didn't understand the context of why she said those words. She held us tight, and we held her tighter, and my heart beat fast.

I didn't want my mother to go. I didn't know what problem she was going through with my stepfather. I only knew that she needed comfort, love, and security.

In the morning, life had returned more to normal, and no one ever spoke of the night before again. But the memories of my mom's fear and insecurity stayed with me long after.

As adults, each of us has our memories of growing up in an alcoholic and dysfunctional family. While growing up, when we needed security and love in our lives, we might have gotten the opposite: fear, anxiety, and lack of love.

For me, I found creative ways to adapt and get by, but even decades later, I still deal with insecurity and fear.

It's easy when people advise on how to deal with such problems. But I find that my way of looking at life has been shaped entirely differently than those around me. Often, I feel like I'm an alien walking among humans. Granted, I don't know if it's because of my personality type (INFJ) or growing up in an alcoholic/dysfunctional home or if it's a combination of things.

Yet I do know this. I am not alone. I know that others feel lost, insecure, and deal with anxiety.

I also know that there are proven ways (for me, at least) to help myself in troubled times. The triggers for my insecurity could be anything from work problems, sickness in my family, to fear about a new challenge.

Instead of retreating into myself, I like to think of a safety net that I've built under me.

I can talk to a therapist, a trusted friend/loved one, listen to music, write in my journal, go for a walk/run, or simply just sit on a bench and enjoy a sunset. I have learned over time what I can do to help me when I'm feeling insecure and worried.

If I have learned anything over the years, it's that I am not weak for being vulnerable. To say that I struggle with insecurity or am anxious, does not make me inferior or damaged. Instead, I like to own who I am, and the act of writing those words gives me power.

What you shine a light on cannot hurt you.

Speaking truth helps free me.

It's funny because, as a man, I grew up being told that "men show strength and never weakness." But that's not true. Maybe it's what some people think, but I never found any of those coping mechanisms to work for me.

Honesty, reflection, and building a support network have helped.

There is no shame in writing that I struggle and have insecurities and fears.

I do not want my children to think that I have it all together and am Superman. I'm not.

I'm flawed, and I'm me.

Just like you. No one else on this planet is exactly like you. Your story, life, and journey are yours and yours alone.

I am not here to tell you what to do. I can't know what will or will not work for you. But I can share what has helped me and share that with you.

What you decide to do in your life is your choice because it's your life.

I think the beauty and power in that statement are so freeing.

It's easy for me to say that you are special and one-of-a-kind.

But do you know it?

If not, what will you do about that?

DAY 67: RECLAIM YOUR POWER

In early 2017, I attended a training session to learn more about activism. I had never participated in a meeting like that before, but I had decided to volunteer and didn't know where to start. More than one hundred people showed up for the event.

I found myself grouped with four other strangers, and we introduced ourselves, sat down at our table, and were ready to learn. We had pens, notepads, and our thinking caps on.

A facilitator kicked off the training session with a simple exercise. Each table received one poster-sized blank sheet of paper and a handful of colored markers.

Our instructions: "Draw the world that you'd like to live in."

That seemed pretty straightforward.

My teammates and I talk about the need for healthcare, so we drew a big hospital, then a river, and some beautiful trees. We then added a school, a city, and started filling in the rest of our perfect society.

Suddenly, from across the large (but packed) room, we heard people crying out. We ignored the disruption and kept working in our beautiful city.

Then I noticed a guy walking up to a table near ours, and he stopped to look at the drawing that people had made and ripped one of the four corners off. He didn't say a word and just went on. The stunned team cried out and started to patch together the damage that had been done.

Distracted for a bit, I sensed someone nearby and looked up to see a young woman come to our table, glance down, and then tear off the bottom right corner of our drawing. We had just lost our hospital.

I looked over at my teammates, and the guy next to me started drawing another hospital to replace the missing one.

I helped draw some more pictures, and louder

cries came from the back of the room, then the front and a line of destruction rippled from table to table. I watched as three people walked from table to table, ripping people's papers to shreds.

One group hid their drawing underneath their table, but the young woman reached down, grabbed a section, and ripped a big piece off their sheet of paper.

I turned away just in time to see a guy stop at our table, grab the center of our drawing, and pull it up. We fought to hold onto the picture, but he quickly crumbled it up and ripped it to pieces.

The cries from the audience grew louder, and the facilitator yelled, "Stop!"

The three disruptors in the crowd froze, but the facilitator went over to one table and pointed at the team. "Everyone, take a look at this group."

I stood up so that I could see better and then realized what the team had done. The individuals at the table had locked arms and leaned in to create a human shield to protect their drawing.

I watched and realized that the strategy had never crossed my mind.

The facilitator turned around to face all of us and said, "There are more than a hundred of you and only three disruptors. What would have happened if each table would have locked arms and created a barrier to keep the disruptors out?" He let his words sink in and looked at every one of us and added, "I have power. You have power. We have power."

I woke up that day.

For a long time, I had looked at myself as being a victim. I grew up in an alcoholic family, we didn't have a lot of money, and I had to overcome so much.

But that's not the whole story. The victim and challenges I went through were part of a story that I told myself, and that limited me.

I have power.

I can write books, blog posts, create podcasts. I can share my story.

You have power.

You can define your worth and be your creator of whatever you imagine.

We have power.

This is the kicker. We are not alone. By

building communities, we can connect and build a protective shield over what we know is precious.

Instead of letting others go through our lives and rip up our beautiful drawings, we can work together to protect and grow.

How?

Let's build a community together.

Join the Let Go and Be Free private Facebook group (https://facebook.com/groups/letgoandbe), and together we'll build a city, brick by brick. If you join, be sure to share a story and say hello.

DAY 68: REFILL YOUR CUP WITH MUSIC

My first memories of music are of my mom putting on The Who's *The Who by Numbers* and playing their song "Squeeze Box." I remember her taking the album out of the sleeve, putting it on the record player, and then blasting the song.

She then picked me up, and we danced around the room.

No matter how difficult and dark my mom's life was with being in an abusive marriage, she used music to elevate her. She would smile, laugh, and sing as loud she could. Her free-spirited joy and her love of music washed over me and taught me a powerful lesson:

Music heals.

Over the years, my mom shared with me her love of The Beatles, The Rolling Stones, The Who, David Bowie and a whole long list of musicians. And I took that love of music and incorporated it into my own life.

Music is a window to my soul. I play music to become alive with how I feel and who I am. With millions of songs now available at our fingertips through our phones, gone are the days when I had to hunt down and find music.

I remember going to a Tower Records near where I lived and trying to sing a song to the cashier. I did my best to sing a few lines of the song and she looked at me like I had two heads. But the song had wrapped itself around my heart and expressed something that I needed in my life.

So, I went downstairs into the basement of the store and sang as much of the song as I could to another employee. He thought for a minute and said, "That's *Galileo* by The Indigo Girls."

I bought the CD and played that song over and over again.

And so, my love of music continued. Through joy, sorrow, grief, and pain, I've used music as therapy and as a safe way of channeling my emotions so that I could process them, overcome a problem, and move on.

I'm happy that now I don't have to carry a Walkman around with extra AA batteries and cassette tapes to play my favorite songs. As a kid, we had albums, then tapes, and CDs (thankfully I skipped the 8-Track phase) and then mp3s and finally streaming.

I want to share a few songs that have helped me grow to who I am now. Songs that have lifted me up, gave me some hope to see the world beyond today and refilled my cup.

The first song that I think of is The Beatles' "Getting Better." My mom grew up with The Beatles and she shared her love of them with me. "Getting Better" helps me see that better days are coming and this upbeat song helps me get over a dark day. I've sung that song many, many times over the years—after breakups, in hard spots in relationships or just for myself. I love the song because of its upbeat tempo.

The next song I wanted to share isn't on Spotify. Though there are tens of millions of songs on the service, some groups haven't worked out contracts with Spotify yet. However, I did find Sweet Honey in the Rock's "Wanting Memories" on YouTube. If you are not familiar with this song, I urge you to stop reading and play the video.

"Wanting Memories" came into my life almost 25 years ago. A friend of mine played the song for me and I listened in silence. She shared with me that it helped her deal with the passing of her mother.

When I hear this song, it transports me to another place. There are so many wonderful parts to this song and I really get choked up when I listen to it.

I'm reminded that I'm connected to something greater than myself, to God, to those who have gone before me and those who will come after me. I feel comforted by "Wanting Memories" and it's a healing salve for me. It's a good cry of a song.

The next song "Hollow in the Ferns" is from the movie *Far from the Madding Crowd* that came out back in 2015, starring Carey Mulligan. The movie is based on Thomas Hardy's fourth novel of the same name. "Hollow in the Ferns" is a song about awakening. The cover of the album sets the scene nicely: Carey Mulligan is in the woods with a soldier she has feelings for but isn't quite ready to take the leap to admit her desire for him.

The song's strings capture that curiosity and awakening in a way that transcends where I'm at and whatever I'm doing. I like listening to this song as loud as I can and to listen for the echoes from the room where the violins were recorded. There's something about the emotional uplifting feeling within this song that helps me when I'm having a rough day.

The next song is from the motion picture The Piano. "The Heart Asks Pleasure First" is a stable of my early 20s. Michael Nyman uses the piano to capture the soul's longing and hope for love. Holly Hunter and a young Anna Paquin won Oscars for their performances in Jane Campion's movie and Nyman's soundtrack cemented the inner emotional turmoil of a young window in a way that is transformative.

I haven't heard that song in many years and as I played it while writing this book, I had a big smile on my face. The song reminds me of days long gone by, love past and of my awakening as an individual.

With my growing understanding that music

could be medicine for my soul, I gravitated toward songs that would be upbeat, positive and help me define my story. Peter Gabriel's "Shaking the Tree" is a song that I play for the women in my life. I think of what they suffered through in their lives and how they still pushed onward. It's a song that reminds me that the world isn't about me. I wouldn't be where I am today if it were not for the sacrifices that my mother made for my brother and me.

I just wouldn't. She could have decided to stay married to my father. She could have given up, but she didn't. She chose to take action and to leave. And she used music to help her in life. When we moved into my grandparents' house, I remember how my mom would go into the basement, turn the stereo up and sing as loud as she could to music. She exorcised her hurt and pain through music.

Now I'm going to take a leap on this next song. I really like Kesha's music and I'll get down to her "Boogie Feet." Sometimes you just need a song that gets you dancing and to sing along. Can I dance well? No. (My friends used to joke with me and call me "hyper hips" when I danced.) Can I sing? No, not really. But I get up and sing anyway. Moving and singing along to "Boogie Feet" is just pure bliss.

I've listened to Kesha's *Rainbow* album over and over and I tip my hat to her. I love this song and I'm on team #FreeKesha. I believe her and pray that she will win her freedom to make her own music under another (or her own) label.

My last song for today is a new one. My teenage son was taking a shower earlier this week, and I heard him playing (very loudly) a song that I didn't recognize.

I caught up with my son later, and he told me that he was listening to Dana Williams' "Hard."

Sometimes a song comes into your life because you need it. It's almost like the universe is sending you a telegram (ah, that's dated)—or a text.

I've only been listening to this song for the last few days, and it's caused me to reflect. I am hard on myself and worse, I expect those around me to have such high standards that it's impossible for them no matter how hard they try.

That's the truth, and it's a hard truth.

Growing up in an alcoholic/dysfunctional family meant that I took on the behaviors of those around me. I became hyper responsible and that put a nice wall around me. Maybe it's time I let that wall down and not be as hard on myself.

See what music can do?

Open your mind, allow you to see beyond the here and now and present truths to you that maybe you didn't want to quite admit.

So, these are some of the songs that help me. What songs do you use to refill your cup?

DAY 69: BREAK OUT OF FEELING TRAPPED

I woke up in the middle of the night with my heart beating fast. A secret fear of being abandoned had taken hold of me. Over the years, the dream has taken on several different forms.

I'm in a classroom, and the teacher comes in and surprises us with a test. I feel unprepared and know no one around me. Or I'm back at an old job in retail. I'm behind the counter, and there's a big sale taking place with dozens of customers waiting for me to ring up their purchases. But I don't remember how to use the cash register, and people are counting on me. Or maybe I'm at a job, and the location of where I sit has been changed. Everyone is acting normal, but I can't find where

I'm supposed to go. I'm stressed, worried, and afraid. I'm then told to go to human resources, and all becomes crystal clear to me. I'm being let go.

In each of those nightmares, I feel powerless. I'm in a pressured situation and am trying to work within a system but don't have the right information to succeed.

How do I overcome it?

First, I admit that I'm struggling and going through a difficult time.

One of my biggest fears is that someone or something has power over me, and I'm trapped in some system that I can't solve or break out.

To deal with this problem, after I admit that I'm going through a rough time, I ask myself: "Is it true?"

I might not have all the information available to me. The type of stress dreams that I have can also be triggered by life events. If you're waiting for a result of a medical test, that situation can also trigger this fear.

If there's a situation that you're going through, but you can't control the outcome, then I fall back on the Serenity Prayer. "God, grant me the serenity to accept the things I cannot change, the courage to change the things I can, and wisdom to know the difference."

We all have limited time and energy.

If I spin my wheels trying to solve a problem that's not solvable, then I'm at a dead-end and keep banging against a wall. I'll never get out. I'll stay trapped.

The tricky thing is understanding that being stuck is not always true.

I could choose not to take the test in the dream. Or I could walk out of the store with all the customers.

Whatever the situation, each of us has a choice. Yes, we don't always have control in our lives. We can't choose to get sick or for an accident to happen to us. But how we deal with that problem is critical to our well-being.

Six years ago, I tore my Achilles' tendon and had a cast on for six weeks. I had to figure out how to get to work each day and navigate through the house when I couldn't put any pressure on my left foot.

Was it true that I was in pain and had a long road of recovery? Yes.

Could I change the situation on my own? No. Full recovery took me six months.

So, what did I do?

I hung up a note on my monitor that said: "Be positive."

I didn't just forget about the pain and suffering I had to go through. But I found that facing adversity with a positive outlook helped me immensely rather than always thinking negatively. I learned a lot about myself during those six months. Being unable to do the most essential things was hard—as was asking for help more often.

I survived and then thrived.

If you feel trapped, you're never alone.

Who can you go to for help?

DAY 70: LONGING TO BELONG

I remember being picked on as a kid and laughed at because I wore gold sneakers to school. I had begged my mom and grandfather not to wear them, but they were bought used at a flea market, and that was all we could afford.

I knew that my classmates would make fun of me. I just knew it.

I went to school and then put my gold sneaks on for gym class. We had track that day, and my classmates picked on me mercilessly. I did my best to tune them out, but it was hard to do knowing that I wore used sneakers. Granted, it shouldn't have mattered, but I was only 10 years old.

By that time in my life, kids picked on me because I wore glasses, was smart (but wouldn't help them cheat on tests), was super skinny, and then I wore golden sneakers in 6th grade.

The laundry list of things that my family and I were different from other families just grew and grew. I didn't have a father in my life, lived with my grandparents, and we didn't have a lot of money.

I just wanted to fit in. I didn't want to stand out and be different. I knew that I was different enough on the inside. I also knew that I saw the world differently than others.

I could write up a story in a blink of an eye and often looked inward. All of these differences put a barrier between me and the kids my age.

I tried so hard to fit in, but I just wanted to belong. I wanted to find a group of similar kids who had gone through what I had and had that unspoken connection.

Back in the '80s, we didn't have the internet or tools to connect with people. I had my three friends on the block, and that was it.

Even now that I'm older, there are still times when I feel like an outsider and that I don't fit into a group. I feel like a third wheel, and yet there are other times that I just click with some people.

I've heard people talk about "finding your tribe" and the importance of that. On the one hand, I think that's important to do, but I also think it's necessary that we step outside our comfort zone and interact with others different than ourselves.

Not everyone thinks and feels like I do, and that's a good thing.

Over the years, I have built up a network of friends who I trust and feel a sense of belonging with in life. We just get each other and give each other space to be.

Have you ever felt disconnected and longed to be part of something bigger than yourself?

What do you do when you feel that way?

For me, I like to start with the basics. If I'm not accepting of myself, then there's no way others can accept me. I focus first on my self-esteem and take care of my own needs. When I feel grounded and sure of myself, then I can connect with others.

I look at it this way: If I'm hungry, tired, or angry, how can I be a good friend to anyone? First I need to take care of myself. If I'm having a problem, then I need to take care of myself or get help.

As a kid and a teenager, I longed to be taken into a group and loved. I so wanted that.

But what I didn't understand back then is that the key to belonging starts with the self first.

If I embrace myself and love myself for all my quirks and faults, then others will truly see me. And yes, even with gold sneakers on.

DAY 71: LIFE ISN'T FAIR

Life isn't fair. So what? What's new?

We can choose to look at things from either a positive perspective or a negative one. We can see ourselves as a victim or as a self-rescuer.

The choice is up to us.

I grew up in Philadelphia that's one of the largest cities in the United States of America and was raised in a middle-class family. When put into perspective, my challenges pale in comparison to others. Over the years that I have authored my fiction books, I have had readers write to me and share the physical and financial challenges they struggle with on a day to day basis.

For those of us who grew up in an alcoholic

family, I think that it's a lot easier for us to remain insecure. And it's easy to blame our alcoholic or dysfunctional parents or relatives for the problems we have today. But I want to be clear: I'm not saying that our problems aren't severe. No, I don't mean that at all.

What I am saying is that we have suffered and gone through dark times (maybe some of you are still struggling). The question is: What are each of us going to do about it?

We can complain and continue to complain but not take any action to solve our problems. The act of complaining gives us the ability to voice our issues to those who will lend us a sympathetic ear. But how do we raise ourselves up and out of the mire?

It's not easy.

Last year I met a man who has cerebral palsy and decided to go to college. Even though it's difficult for him to talk, walk, or write, he didn't give up on his dream. I listened to him tell a story about how he's often treated, and it moved me. When he had first started college, he didn't know how to get to one of his classes on campus. He went up to a teacher and asked for help, but the teacher thought he was begging for money and shooed him away.

Still, even though he had been mistreated, he did not give up. He continued to go to classes, at his pace and is achieving his dreams. He could easily say, "Life isn't fair" and throw his arms up in despair.

But he hasn't done that. He struggles and works hard to do the best that he can do each day. He is not a victim. He's become a symbol of heroism on campus because of how hard he works toward his dream.

If we limit ourselves to be victims and less than deserving, how will we ever succeed?

Take a moment, stop and think, what is holding you back and why?

And then, take one step forward toward your goal. Even if it's a baby step, one step is better than none.

DAY 72: IF NOT TODAY, THEN WHEN?

If not today, then when will you start?

To climb the mountain, get the new job, look for love, get divorced, leave your current job, write that book or live the life you always dreamed.

When?

Tomorrow or the day after that or maybe next year?

We do not know how long we have here. We just don't.

I am scared shitless these days. I have major choices to make, and I'm afraid that I'll make the wrong decision. I'm afraid that I might fail. I'm afraid that I'll disappoint those who count on me.

And yet, I need to try.

There is that moment between making a decision and not. It's a safe space in that you can think about taking the first step without doing it and gives you a buffer of time of feeling good about *thinking* about then deciding.

Thinking about taking action and doing it are entirely two different things.

It's comfortable to think about the idea but never start. The fear of failure or rejection can overwhelm.

You are not alone.

I decided to write this book because I wanted to challenge myself each day. The mechanics of the task are challenging: I need to come up with a topic, write about it in a short amount of time each morning, and do all the nitty-gritty work on the back end to make my writing go live to the world.

I am now 72 days in. It doesn't matter if someone reads my posts or not. Yes, I'd like more people to read my work. But I committed myself to try and to put my feelings out there.

I wanted to write about my fears, anxiety, and my weaknesses—to lay them bare for all to see (and hopefully identify with).

If I don't take action today, why not?

Why is the fear so great that it would stop me

from doing what I always longed and dreamed of doing? Is the fear and pain of rejection so great that it can paralyze me and make me feel small?

I have known failure. I have been ridiculed. I have not gotten the job. I have lost love.

But each time, I choose to get up and try again. Try a new way, a different way, a way to achieve my dreams.

The critical voice inside my head says that I'm delusional. I'm not special. I'm just going to fail like everyone else, and then I'll regret putting my neck out and trying.

Have you ever felt this way?

What is stopping you from embracing your greatest dream? Money? Time? Ability?

I talk a big game about trying and taking steps to achieve my life's goal.

I believe that, no matter how difficult our childhood, we can use imaginative stories to heal ourselves and lead lives filled with love and hope. I believe it's my goal to share stories with people all around the world and to listen.

What do you want to do?

If you're standing in the spot between listening to your fear and taking the first step, what will change you inside to take action?

One day we will look back on our lives and see all that we have done and all we will leave behind. What is it within your heart that would hurt so much that you could not live with that burden on you?

Whatever that is, then today's the day.

Take a leap of faith and try.

Bridges to the future are not built in a day. They are created piece by piece. To start a journey means exactly that: To begin. It might take years of hard work to achieve our dreams, but if we don't start today, then when?

Today is the day.

Today is **your** day.

DAY 73: PERFECTIONISM IS THE ENEMY

Why?

Nothing in this world is perfect. I am flawed. You are flawed. We all are flawed. Waiting to create the perfect piece of art or to say the most appropriate thing to solve a problem, it's just not going to happen.

I think that perfectionism is fear in disguise.

We have an easy out by saying that we don't want to try because we want something to be as perfect as it can be.

But the day that we reach perfection is never going to come.

I wrote my first novel when I was 16 years old. I then rewrote it and tried for almost twenty years to get the book published. I kept tinkering with the book and rewriting it because I kept looking for an agent or a publisher for validation. I wanted them to say, "You have a great piece of art here. Let's publish it, and we'll sell lots of copies for you."

That dream never came to be.

However, I did self-publish the book. Did I sell lots of copies? No. It was my first book, and I had a lot to learn.

After I published the first book, I realized that I could write another book and then another. I know this might sound weird that I didn't understand that I could write another book. Just saying those words now sounds odd to me as well.

I grew up in an era in which you wrote a fantasy book, and then you published the sequel. In my head, I had convinced myself that I HAD to sell the first book, and then I'd write a sequel.

I had never considered that I could just write another book that had nothing to do with the first one.

I could free myself of the past and create a new path.

Take the word "book" out of this story and replace it with a job, a relationship, a problem, whatever.

What are you stuck on?

Ask yourself if it has anything to do with perfectionism. Be truthful as no one is looking at your answer. It's only for you to know.

If you could let go and just try something and become unstuck, what would that be?

Got it?

Then get started.

DAY 74: GIVE YOURSELF A BREAK

I don't mean just take a moment to stop working on yourself. Sure, that's important but I'm talking about a different use of the turn of phrase. By "Give yourself a break," I mean: Stop being down on yourself and beating yourself up.

I am a harsh critic of myself.

If I make a mistake and do wrong to someone, I feel bad and guilty. But here's the thing: I don't have a time machine, and neither do you. There's nothing I can do to go back and fix the things I've said and done in the past. It's impossible.

I'm always reminded of my mom. When I would do something as a kid, and I apologize, she would say to me, "I don't want you to say, 'I'm sorry.' Those words don't mean anything to me. Your father used to say them to me all the time, and he would still do horrible things."

Now say what you will about my mom's tactics in trying to teach me a lesson. As an adult, I understand her more. She didn't want me to use empty words and not change my behavior. She wanted me to be contrite and repeat the same behavior that got me in trouble as a kid.

I am not perfect, and I make all sorts of mistakes each day. I say and do the wrong things; I can be selfish, act in anger, and remain inert when acting would be best. I'm flawed, just like every other person.

For me, the lesson for me to learn is to strive to be a good person, and that starts with being good to myself.

Stop being down on yourself.

Getting caught in a mind loop on worrying how you could have said something better yesterday or done something different five years ago, it's wasted energy.

The most important thing is the here and now.

What can you do today that will be healthy for you?

What actions can you take to ensure that you are being balanced in your life and are treating yourself well?

For today, how can you treat others with dignity and respect?

It's easy for me to relive the past and get caught in a loop by worrying about what I should have done differently. Letting go of the past, owning up to my mistakes, and then forging a better path by my actions in the present will help heal me.

Give yourself a break.

Take some time to ease up on berating yourself. Seriously.

There are enough problems that we have in the world than to pile on by being our own worst enemy.

Flip the switch and give yourself comfort and love.

I look at it this way: In the middle of the night, when we wake up and are struggling with fear, anxiety, guilt, or depression, the simple thought that we are worth it can help. A simple thought of positivity and love to propel us toward a path of healing.

If you're struggling, reach out. See a therapist. Talk with a trusted friend. Take a step forward that will help you.

I wish for you a day that you can be calm, at peace, and in love (with yourself).

DAY 75: EMBRACING THE FEAR WITHIN

Overcoming fear is not easy. It could be fear of change, the unknown, or feeling stuck and not knowing where to go and how to escape and move forward.

When I was a kid, I tried hard to outrun my past. I was a good student, studied hard, and did everything I could to do the right thing. I didn't do drugs or drink. I tried to be the best I could be.

I promised myself that I would not grow up to be like my father.

I would be different and lead a life filled with goodness and light.

Life is complicated, and as you grow older,

you see the different paths in front of you, and you have choices.

One of the things that harmed me the most is that I tried so hard to cut out parts of my personality. By trying **not** to be like my father and rebel against that, I set myself up in a trap.

The behavior patterns and how I react to stressful environments are carved into me. The challenge is that instead of trying to get rid of who I am, that I need to embrace it. This might seem like the most twisted logic.

I think of it this way: When my kids were little, I learned that when they were upset, they would cry. If I overreacted and tried to calm them, that only reinforced their behavior. Instead, I would let them know that I loved them, was there for them, and remained a steady presence in their lives. They realized that they were going to be okay. A lightning storm might wake them up in the middle of the night, and I would hear them cry, so I would check in on them to show my love and support.

The same is true of the fear and angst within. By embracing that, owning it, and shining a light on our fears, they lessen. Hiding and trying to ignore our fears are not only self-sabotaging, but they can debilitate us.

If we support and love, the dark and as well as our light parts, we step on firm ground.

The foundation of what we built our lives on is made up of our habits, the people we choose to surround ourselves with, along with how we treat others and ourselves.

Instead of trying to hide from our fears, or worse stressing out about them all the time, it's best to own up to them, shine a light on them, talk about them (to a therapist, loved one), and grow.

What happened to us may be horrible and filled with deep trauma and getting through those moments takes time and patience.

The first step is to gather ourselves together and embrace the fear.

Yes, it might be scary and hard.

But step by step, we can do it. Together.

DAY 76: ACCEPT A DOUGHNUT

A few years back, I went to see Amanda Palmer on her tour. She had just released her The Art of Asking book and had been in the news because she had raised more than a million dollars on Kickstarter to help fund her most recent album. If you're not familiar with Palmer, she's a musician who is outspoken and is open to embracing her fans.

Some might critique her ways, but I find her artistry welcoming.

An Amanda Palmer concert was unlike any I have ever been to before. First, she would tell a story and then play a song. Many in the audience had seen her multiple times, and they knew that at the end of the concert, she would stick around for hours talking with her fans.

I had expected that I'd go to the concert, there would be an opening act, she would play songs, finish her set, and then come back for an encore. Instead, she told stories about her life and then wove in songs throughout the night.

During the concert that I went to, se shared a story about a doughnut that's stuck with me. At one time in her life, someone had offered her a doughnut, and she declined. The story she told morphed into a symbolic doughnut of opportunity. Each day we are given chances to try something different, embrace a new choice, and reach toward our full potential. Her advice to us: "Always take the doughnut."

I started thinking about her advice and realized that I could say "yes" more to opportunities and overcome my fears. Even at a simple level, I could be different. When I get off the train and see a young kid selling lemonade, I "take the doughnut" and buy a glass (and give a tip). The time when a colleague asked me to speak about social media at a local events planner meeting, I agreed and stepped out of my comfort zone to do something different.

What doughnuts are you being offered each day that you could accept?

Is it fear that's holding you back by taking a chance?

Why is that?

The only amendment that I've made to Amanda Palmer's advice is adding in a question: "Is it healthy for me?"

Some opportunities aren't, and I take stock of my mental, physical, and emotional well-being before I agree.

I have run marathons, volunteered at homeless shelters, given talks at conferences, and a whole slew of other fantastic life experiences because I said yes.

What about you?

DAY 77: UNPLUG AND GO FOR A NATURE WALK

I grew up not too far from a huge park. When I became old enough, my friends and I would get on our bikes and drive all through the woods. The trails were great for our dirt bikes, and we spent hours in the woods.

We'd stop at the waterfalls, park our bikes, and lose track of time as we'd skip rocks over the water. Or we'd do stupid stuff like putting a large fallen branch into the creek to see it go over the falls.

I miss those days. Even though I lived in one of America's largest cities, the entrance to the park was less than a mile away.

Now things are a bit harder for me to get out into nature.

Modern life can be overwhelming with our phones, TVs, and the internet. We're almost always plugged in these days and have some sort of information being sent at us. And even if you don't use your phone all the time, the effects of our day-to-day routines can be draining on us.

When I get that way, I unplug and head out for a walk.

In the summertime, I am lucky enough to be near Longwood Gardens. I can walk through miles of beautiful paths lined with flowers, but my favorite part is going to the fields in the unpopulated section of the gardens. You can walk around the field and do some bird watching and get lost in nature.

Why would you want to do this?

About two years ago, I heard about forest bathing and its benefits.

To overcome stress, anxiety, and worry, I have found that getting out into nature and walking can be healing. When I give myself time to relax and to enjoy the world around me, I find the connection with the outdoors to be a soothing balm for my soul.

If you're struggling with mobility, can you find a place to take an electric scooter to get your around (a zoo, a garden, etc.)?

Take your phone, put it away, turn off the TV and the internet, and go enjoy outside.

Watch the sky, smell the flowers, and just be.

DAY 78: YOU'VE FAILED. NOW WHAT?

I have failed more times than I can remember. But a failure that stings is writing my *Ahab's Daughter* book. I woke up early writing before work, struggled to get the funds together to have the cover made, and then launched the book, and it flopped.

I received positive reviews on the book, but my launch and marketing didn't bring in new readers. I launched a new series out to the world, and no one seemed to care.

The months of hard work that I put into the book went seemingly down the drain.

When we fail, we can throw our hands up in disgust and give up, or we can learn from our mistakes and get up and try again.

Maybe you've had a failed relationship, just got divorced, are estranged from your kids, lost your job, or had a major medical setback—the question is: What are you going to do now?

I waited for many years for others to validate me as a writer. I wanted people to run to me with open arms to publish my books and got rejected time and time again. I even questioned whether I should give up writing.

I used to joke with my wife and tell her that I could get a minimum wage job on the side and make more money than I do with writing. But here's the thing: J.K. Rowling was turned down by 12 publishing houses before she could see her Harry Potter books get published. The book *Chicken Soup for the Soul* was rejected 144 times. Kathryn Stockett's *The Help* was rejected 60 times from various agents.

Where have you failed?

Maybe it's with a personal goal and has nothing to do with a job or getting a book published. I've heard people tell their stories about how they picked up drinking or using drugs again and how they felt gutted with the struggles they have with addiction.

The same holds true: When you fail, what are you going to do?

Give up? Complain and not act?

Or get back up, dust off your knees, and get to work again?

When I fail, I take stock of what happened and learn what I could have done better. I take that to heart and then apply that to how I'll move on.

Sometimes the failure is a blessing in disguise. One door closes, and another opens. But we often only see the few feet in front of us and not the full journey of our lives.

If failure comes your way, embrace it and feel how it hurts, but then let it go.

Write another book. Try for another job. Go out with friends if you've been dumped. Give compassion and empathy to a friend.

We don't know what the future will bring. We can't see that.

But we have a choice to go on, keep trying, grow, shift, evolve, and get up.

I invite you to think of failure as an opportunity. Spin the coin around and see the opportunity that presents itself.

Is getting up and trying again hard? You bet it is.

But that's the beauty of it. What you learn will make you that much stronger.

DAY 79: SELF-SABOTAGE AND FEAR OF SUCCESS

You're just about to reach out, grab the gold ring to win the prize, and then your world crashes down all around you.

I exaggerate, but maybe not as much as you might think.

In growing up in an unstable household with alcohol, drugs, and dysfunction, we've become accustomed to instability. It's what we know.

Someone pushes our buttons, we react, and the circle of anger/fear/dysfunction goes round and round in an unending circle.

The stories we tell ourselves can be clouded with fear:

"I'm not good enough." "I don't deserve that." "Nobody loves me."

All of the fear, pain, and scarcity can be wrapped up in knots within us and we go about our lives doing the best we can. Just when we are about to succeed, we pull back, or worse, self-sabotage.

But why?

The pain/fear that we know is easier to handle than the unknown.

Change is hard. If there's no way for us to know for sure whether the choice we could take would be better for us, it might seem easier to stay where we are.

I've made decisions in my life that have been for the best and for the worst. That's life. There isn't a way to know what's going to be the best outcome.

But if we block our own path to success, we become our own enemy. In a way, we are repeating the destructive behaviors that we grew up with in our households.

The question is: What are you going to do about it?

Today.

Not five weeks from now, or some undisclosed day in the future.

Today.

One of the most powerful lessons that I've learned is that each of us has the power to change our fate. We truly do have power.

If we see our lives as empty, negative, or that we're the victim, then we perpetuate a line of thinking that restrains and holds us back from living to our greatest potential.

But what if we flipped those thoughts, changed them, and realized that we can make a different choice and embrace opportunity. We can be happy and enjoy all that life has to offer.

Sound too woo-woo to you?

If we embrace the possibilities of today and flip the switch in our thinking, what opportunities could present themselves to us?

Instead of negativity, what if we said, "Yes"?

DAY 80: OVERCOMING DEEP FEAR

I'm afraid. I'm writing this with a heavy weight on me and fear that I may fail. I'm afraid that if I listen to myself and follow my instincts that I'm delusional and will not succeed.

I'm afraid that I'll not be able to put food on the table for my family and that I should just shut up and go along with the flow.

But there's a voice inside, the "me" that's always been there. I saw and went through a lot in growing up. These experiences have shaped me to be the man I am today (for better or worse).

I feel this fear to try something new and to follow my instincts because I cannot see the outcome. My upbringing was unstable, and I sometimes didn't know where things would wind up at the end of the day.

I'm older now, and I have a choice to make.

I can follow my instincts and be true to myself, or I can go along for the ride and stay quiet.

When you're faced with choices that you're afraid to make, I find that a deep-rooted fear grabs me. The emotion is strong, and I'm pulled back down with memories resurfacing of me as a little kid. Watching the family dynamics playing out and being powerless to do anything to save me.

I kept thinking: "Why do I feel this impending dread?"

The same feeling of dread has risen on me, but here's the thing: If I speak about the fear, shine a light on it, I can name it. I can embrace it and pass through it.

I can overcome my fear.

The challenge, though, is that our emotions aren't a switch. I can't just decide to not feel fear any longer about this topic. The fear ebbs and flows.

Some days I'm fine. But there are others when doubt creeps in, I'm tired and feel spent, and external pressures are hitting me from all sides.

That's when it's a dangerous time.

I know that I'm not the only person who feels this way. I'm writing this so that you can see that I haven't cornered the market on "dispelling fear in 5 easy steps." That's not how real-life works.

Our lives are like quilts makes from the different fabric of our experiences. The light and the dark. The gray and the varied array of a double rainbow.

In the silence of the night, when we are alone, and we wake up from a nightmare, fear grips us. It's at those low points that we need help. We need to fall back on all the tools in our basket to help us through a difficult time.

As unsexy as they might seem, what helps me are:

- Eating right.
- Sleeping enough.
- Meditating daily.
- Sharing freely.

The challenge isn't how to overcome our deep-rooted fears but how to remain balanced in our lives. The fears beat at us when we're tired and drained. I believe it's our job to keep ourselves rested and in good emotional balance.

We need to take care of ourselves. Day in and day out.

Lately, I've been pushing myself too hard and my fears are gaining on me.

Time to pull back, to rest, to heal, and to be.

DAY 81: ARE YOU LIKE DOUBTING THOMAS?

As a Catholic, in school, the nuns would have us read parts of the Bible for classwork. When I read Luke 9:3, I scratched my head: "And he said to them, 'Take nothing for your journey, no staff, nor bag, nor bread, nor money; and do not have two tunics.'"

Jesus asked his disciples to go out into the world and that they didn't need to bring anything with them. They would be okay with food, drink, a place to stay, and wouldn't need any money. I couldn't figure that out.

Why would Jesus say that to his disciples? At 12-years-old, I questioned Jesus' advice and worried about the disciples. I couldn't see how they would survive. What would they do for food? Where would they sleep?

I just didn't get it.

It wasn't until I grew older that I started to understand. The charisma, nurturing, and message of love that the disciples brought with them would win over converts. People would provide for them. The disciples needed to trust that their work would win over hearts and minds.

That's a powerful message.

It's similar to the doubting Thomas part of the Bible when Jesus told him to "Reach here with your finger, and see My hands; and reach here your hand and put it into My side; and do not be unbelieving, but believing."

Thomas does so and believes.

What I like about Luke 9:3 is that the plight of the disciples is much more complicated. When a miracle is right before our eyes, sure, we see it and believe. But like the disciples, we need to find the strength to believe in ourselves.

We need to find the strength to cast off doubt even when others are criticizing us.

We are human and make mistakes every day. From the smallest to the biggest of problems, life happens, and we stumble.

But imagine facing life without the "staff, bag, bread, or money."

What would that mean for you to wake up and face the day with confidence?

How can you believe in yourself today?

What internal struggles hold you back from doing good and being happy?

Think about them, bring them close to you, and then let them go.

Even if it's just one small thing, belief is built bit by bit and taking a leap of faith.

Why not try it today?

Take the leap.

DAY 82: SAYING GOODBYE

I often felt like I didn't have much control in my life as a kid. When my mom and father divorced, I was about 6 years old, and I went from having my room to moving in my grandparents and sharing a room with my younger brother. We got along fine, but then we moved again when our mom remarried.

Leaving my friends was difficult. Then when our mom divorced a second time, and we moved back into my grandparents' house again, I again lost the friends I had made.

But I remember an especially difficult time that I hadn't expected.

When I was 12 years old, my friends and I became friendly with two sisters on our block. They had moved in with their grandparents so that their father could work in the city, but they would move back to Oklahoma. With our living in Philadelphia, Oklahoma might just have been Spain.

My friends and I had a great time with the sisters. We played tag and hung out all the time. We became fast friends. After about a year, the news came that the sisters needed to move back to Oklahoma. I still remember saying goodbye and feeling heartbroken.

The sisters left early on a Saturday morning, and I got up to press my nose against the window and I watched as the big truck parked in front of their house. The movers added all their things into the big truck, and I waved to the sisters one last time.

They left that morning, and a part of me felt broken and sad.

Too many times I had lost friends through moving, but this time it was different because I was left behind.

I saw the sisters about ten years later, and I hardly recognized them. We talked and said hello, but the bond that we had as kids had been broken.

We had not stayed in touch, and the distance had been too great.

Saying goodbye can be difficult. Because I had such instability in my early life, I have a hard time saying goodbye. And yet, nothing lasts forever.

Sometimes letting go and saying goodbye offers other opportunities that we are not able to see in the present moment.

Sometimes we're not ready to say goodbye but have to because someone we love has passed on.

Sometimes we're left behind.

In the end, it all still hurts, and we feel raw inside.

I know that's how I felt.

Time does heal wounds, but some hurt takes months or years to overcome.

And for today, I want to acknowledge that. Saying goodbye is hard for me. It hurts and takes time for me to heal.

None of us know how much time we have with our friends and family.

Go find someone you love and hug them. Tell them how much you love them. And be true.

To yourself and the future.

What we have today is all we have.

DAY 83: MAKE AMENDS WHEN WRONG

No one likes to be wrong. At work, with your spouse, children, or family. But we all make mistakes, and sometimes our behaviors hurt another person.

Each day I take time to go through how I've acted, and I reflect on the things that I could have done better. I then actively work to make amends to anyone I have hurt.

It seems easy enough, right?

Sometimes though, emotions get in the way. When tensions are tight, and you can't see eye-to-eye with someone, I recommend taking some time to cool off. Then come back together, listen to the person, and see if you can build a bridge to solve the problem.

What I'm seeing in the world right now is that we lack empathy, authenticity, and the willingness to listen. One side goes in thinking that they are right, and the other side does the same. Neither side is willing to listen or to compromise an inch.

Underneath the surface, I have a moral code that I follow. I do my best to be open-minded and have always followed the Golden Rule: "Do unto others as you would have them do unto you."

That's gotten me through lots of problems, time and time again. However, there's another way. Dave Kerpen has come up with the Platinum Rule. In his book, *The Art of People,* he recommends that we "treat other people as they would like to be treated."

Everyone is different, and when we're looking to make amends, why not treat someone **the way they want** rather than what works for us?

It's a radical idea, isn't it?

The next time you're looking to make amends to someone for something that you've done, talk with them, actively listen to what they need, and then treat them as they'd like.

If we're truly sorry, then flipping things and

being open to showing someone we are sorry and doing better makes all the difference.

It's not always what we want and how we see the world. I know that I'm guilty of this myself.

What would happen if we all treated others the way that they wanted rather than what we impose on them?

DAY 84: YOU DESERVE IT

"You deserve it."

What do you think of when you read those words? Is your first thought a negative one on how something bad has happened, and you think that deep down, you deserve the bad thing that just happened?

Those of us who grew up in an alcoholic or dysfunctional family often internalize the problems we see around us. Somehow, for some reason, we deserve that bad thing that happened.

But let's flip that thought pattern around. Try this on for size:

"You worked hard. You deserve the promotion."

"You are so thoughtful. You deserve all the good friends you have."

Coming out of our shell can help us see the world around us in a different (and more positive) way. Yesterday I went to an event with more than twenty people packed into the living room. I stood alone for a bit and had an introverted idea cross through my head: "Alert! Alert! Backup and go into hiding."

But I pushed through that and engaged the woman sitting across from me. It's easy to take out our phones and ignore the world around us so that we can feel more secure. Or we can create situations where we're comfortable and safe.

The world we create can quickly become a prison. If we do not reach out to others, people may leave us alone. If we think that we are not worth it, why would others think differently?

We manifest our destiny. If we believe we aren't worth it, how much simpler is it to make that a self-fulfilling prophecy?

The challenge is to see ourselves as worthy. The bad stuff that happened in the past might have helped define who we are today but that's not the totality of our makeup. We can see ourselves as victims or survivors.

Do you see the difference?

DAY 85: FAKE IT UNTIL YOU MAKE IT?

"Fake it until you make it."

I've always hated that phrase. I always thought it was like saying: "Keeping smiling, and you'll feel happy." It doesn't matter if you're going through depression, grief, or another big life-changer; you'll be fine if you just pretend.

I don't like pretending that I feel good, or I know what I'm doing.

That has never worked for me.

I like to flip things around a bit and focus on what isn't and is working. Enacting lasting changes in life take a great deal of effort and time.

For me, I would much rather try to make it each day. I focus on using the current skills I have to get me through the problem I'm having or to work toward making a change in my life.

Instead of just flipping a switch in my head to pretend that I am "making it," I would much rather take a baby step toward the better day. When I'm tackling a big problem, I know that it takes time.

When I trained for a marathon or wrote my first book, I didn't fake it. I realized that I needed to take the few first steps. For the marathon, that meant I ran around the block twice. Then months later, I ran around my daughter's school twice. I then ran a mile, then two, and eventually, my first 5K (3.1 miles).

My friends challenged me to then run a 10-miler run in Philadelphia with around 37,000 people in it. I trained for that race, then my friends asked me to do a half-marathon one month later (that's 13.1 miles), and I did that. Two years of steady running later, I trained for a marathon (26.2 miles), and I did it.

I didn't fake anything. I started badly, had no clue what I was doing, but I began to eat healthier, focus on my water intake, set a consistent running schedule, subscribed to Runner's World magazine, and talked with my fellow friends who ran. I learned about my gait, the proper running shoe, what stretches helped me deal with pain after my long runs, and some not so fun stuff like the importance of using body glide to help with chaffing to prevent any red marks on my thighs.

Going from couch to crossing the finish line of my first marathon took years of hard work. It was a journey. I learned things, I failed at things, I pieced together a plan and changed my worldview to go from "I'll never run a marathon" to "I've run three."

I don't like to fake things.

I prefer being open and authentic. If I don't know what I'm doing, I'll say it. I will try my best and then learn from what didn't work. I'll build on my experiences and put together a plan to succeed.

The same is true in writing and marketing a book.

Or the time that a girlfriend of mine broke up with me back in graduate school. I felt lost and alone, but slowly I rebuilt my friendships, connected with new people, and took risks by going to new places. Eventually, I met my wife—not because I sat on my sofa being miserable, but I worked hard to build up a new life for myself.

I learned to remember that I am worthy of love.

I didn't fake it. I put in the hard work to get me from point A to point B.

What I like about the gradual journey is the best part: You only need to take one step at a time. Go at your pace but keep getting up and working toward your goal.

What about you?

What do you want to do?

Don't fake it. Just be you.

DAY 86: TRY SOMETHING NEW

When is the last time that you tried something new?

I find that what helps me in life is shaking things up a bit and trying something that's out of my comfort zone.

When I tried my first mud run, I had no idea what I was getting involved in. Friends of mine had invited me to get into running, and I loved it. But when I found a 10K mud run taking place in my area to raise money for MS, I wanted to give it a try. (A mud run is a course that's filled with obstacles and things like mud pits.)

A friend of mine put me in contact with a group, and I showed up on the day of the race, having never met the other ten people on my team before.

I said hello to my team members, and we were off. Within the first mile, I saw an experienced runner slip down a rocky hill, twist his ankle, and knock him out of the race. And then we crossed a small river with a pretty powerful current. We linked arms and helped pull each other across to the other side.

As a team, we finished the difficult course, and it never felt so good to take a shower afterward. I had mud everywhere.

If I hadn't signed up for the race, I would have missed out on a fun experience that helped raise money for a great cause.

Every day we have opportunities to try something new.

The next time you see a kid in your neighborhood selling lemonade, stop, buy one from them, and give a tip.

Sign up for a poetry reading or open mic night.

Go volunteer at a local homeless shelter or another community-centered group.

Read a different type of book than you normally would or see a concert and bring a friend.

The list of activities that you can try is pretty much endless, and each one can teach you:

- How it's important to have fun.
- How new experiences can teach you a lot about yourself.

As a kid, I didn't have many opportunities to get out and do things. I had my friends, and that's about it. I didn't have the option to join the Boy Scouts, never learned to play an instrument, or be in a school play.

I hid within my shell because of how challenging my early life had been. I wanted to hide and be left alone.

I was afraid and didn't want anyone to see me.

Writing became my outlet.

But as I became older, I started to open up and have new opportunities in college. I joined some groups, made friends, and had fun.

Now that I'm an adult, my time is limited. I expect the same might be true for you.

Sit down, write in a journal, and just list ten things that you always wanted to do. Find one within your budget and ability and do it.

Why?

The day-to-day grind of our monotonous activities can trap us and give us a false sense of security.

Break out, think of something fun, and do it.

Even if you fail, it doesn't matter.

Treat yourself to something new.

You might just find an activity that helps heal and center you.

DAY 87: ARE YOU AWAKE?

Don't like what's on TV? Turn it off and make your own movie.

Feel oppressed at your job? Get another one.

Sick of the same old type of books out in the store? Write one of your own.

Disgusted with the news and how everything looks horrible? Volunteer and make a difference in the world.

It's easy to point the finger and say, "that is wrong," but power is self-given. No one is going to come up to you, give you the scepter of might, and say, "You now have the power to go take on the world."

That's not how life works.

But it's funny how we wait for change as though we're not able to make decisions for ourselves.

I know that I've been guilty of a helpless or victim mindset. I have gone through situations and felt powerless to make a change.

The reality is that there are gradations of what can and cannot be changed.

Our role is to recognize what we can change and do it. We can't change how other people feel or what they do. We can try and even work on manipulation and control, but in the long run, we will have lost because those people will eventually catch on to us and leave us.

Better to be honest, open, and work on what you can address in yourself.

If you want to exercise, take small steps to do that. Saying that you don't have enough hours in the day, frankly, is an excuse. I've heard fellow indie authors (who are the mother of several children) tell their stories of writing books and how they make time in their lives to raise their children and write.

Is it easy?

No.

Will sacrifices need to be made?

Sometimes, yes.

Maybe the TV has to be turned off, or you get up an hour earlier.

But I would ask you this: What is holding you back?

What dream have you always wanted to try, but you've let slip by because "you don't have the time" or "you're not ready yet."

See what's around you, pick one thing, and make a difference to do good.

When we point at others or situations for holding us back, we're not allowing ourselves the opportunity to grow.

Yes, it can be scary. And yes, growing can be hard.

But the alternative is far, far worse.

DAY 88: FINDING YOUR TRUE LOVE

Do you want to find your true love?

Someone who will love you through thick and thin. Someone who will be patient with your quirks and faults.

Here's what you do. Take a deep and relaxing breath, release slowly, and look up into a mirror.

There, you've found your true love.

It's you.

It's always been you.

How easy it is to throw ourselves into our jobs, our children, our partners, but many of us don't take the time to foster our deepest and longest relationship—with ourselves.

Take a good long minute to look in the mirror

and take in your reflection in. Lean forward and let the light catch the color in your eye and see the variation there.

You are unique and worthy of love.

Take your energy and funnel it inward. Not to be selfish, greedy, and self-serving, but to embrace all of you, as you are today.

Love yourself with abandon.

Love.

DAY 89: DON'T GIVE UP

Let me put my cards on the table. There are days when I wake up and think, "Why am I doing all this? It's not successful. I'm failing, and I'm not getting where I want to be."

I've had this feeling of failure come upon me, and the easiest thing would be to give up.

I could stop trying to write books. Stop trying to create new works. Just stop trying.

But I want to share a story with you. After a failed relationship, I tried to meet someone new, and things didn't work out. I kept meeting people, but either I liked the person and they didn't like me, or they liked me, and I wasn't really into them.

I tried to see if my friends knew anyone who

they thought I might like, and that didn't work (because my friends didn't know anyone who was still single). I even tried a dating service once, and that didn't work.

The more energy that I put into trying to meet someone, the worse things seemed to be.

Finally, I got to the point in which I remember thinking, "You know what, I give up. I'm just going to do my own thing, and if I meet someone, great. If not, well, there's nothing I can do about it. I'm just going to be me and do my thing."

About two weeks after that, I met my wife.

My daughter recently had a problem in which she wanted to create a video with her friend, but all of them canceled on her at the last minute. She had put a reservation at a local dance studio to film the video, and it all fell apart the night before. I met with my daughter and told her this story:

Twenty-five years ago, I had signed up for a poetry reading at a Borders bookstore. I asked all my friends to come to support me, but one by one, they dropped out. Not on purpose, but because it was during a weeknight and my friends had work, graduate school, and probably a few just didn't want to go.

I had to make a choice: Sit home or go on my own. I chose to go.

I don't remember what poems I read that night, but I remember that all went well. After the poetry reading, a friend of mine was putting away the folding chairs, and I went up to help him. While he and I were talking, a young woman came up to him. She was also his friend. The three of us started chatting, and within 15 minutes, we had made plans to meet in the city on Valentine's day as we were all going to be alone. I took a chance, said I'd go, and the rest is history. Our mutual friend dropped out on the Valentine's day dinner, and I took a risk and went to meet the young woman. Twenty-five years later, she and I are now married and have two children.

I told my daughter this story and got teary-eyed. I asked her to consider that if she gave up and didn't go on the film the video she had planned that she might miss out on a fantastic time. If I had decided not to go to the poetry reading, I wouldn't have met my wife and my kids would never have existed.

My daughter decided to go make her film with her brother and they a good time. No, it wasn't a world-shattering event, but I wanted to share with her an important lesson: Sometimes, everyone bails on us. If we still believe in our dream, then we need to go forward and be brave.

We don't know how far along the path success is or meeting the love of our life or finding an amazing job. We can't see it. It's like we're in the dark and have a candle. We can see a few steps in front of us, but that's it.

When we have faith and keep moving toward our dream, that's when the magic happens.

I wanted so much to meet someone, but I was trying too hard. I met my wife when I went out and took a risk by reading my poetry to a bunch of strangers. Yes, the story would be much more romantic to say that she heard my poetry and loved it. But that's not the truth. She was on the first floor of the bookstore and didn't come up until after the reading was over. But because I didn't stay home and let my dream slip through my fingers, I found myself in the right place at the right time.

I made my own luck.

Each book that I write, each connection I make, each act of volunteering that I perform, or each day I try something new allows me to grow and be one step closer to my goal.

I know that sometimes things look bleak.

But I ask you to consider: If you give up on your dream, you might have done so within steps away from your goal.

I might never have commercial success as a fantasy/science fiction author, but I'll never know that unless I keep trying. I write new books; I take training sessions on marketing. I network with fellow authors. I keep trying. Inch by inch. Day by day. I keep moving forward in life.

What about you?

DAY 90: HELLO, FUTURE YOU

If you grew up in an alcoholic and dysfunctional family like me, thinking about the past might bring up a whole host of bad memories.

I remember feeling powerless as a child and not understanding all that was happening around me. I knew my father had left, and that money was tight so that we needed to move in with my mom's parents, but I didn't fully comprehend the shame and fear I had experienced.

I used my imagination to create a safe space where I could escape and grew up the best I could.

As a kid, I tried to imagine the future and wondered where I would be. What would I grow up to be? Where would I live? I struggled to envision a better day than the present.

Now that I'm an adult, I look back at my childhood and am so thank for all my mom sacrificed for my brother and me.

I was the first one to go to college in my family, and I knew that education would help pull me out of my life and open doors for me in ways that I couldn't truly understand as a kid. But I knew that I wanted a good job and a family.

Now that I'm an adult, when I struggle, I sometimes get caught up in the same loop I'd find myself in as a kid. I'll worry about the future and the unknown. I catastrophize and blow a problem out of proportion.

I recently went on a long run and struggled to get up a long hill. I tuned out and just let my brain wander. Out of nowhere, a thought came to me: "One day a future you will look back on today and smile. He'll know that you were going through a difficult time but that you made it through. You survived and thrived."

As I chugged up the hill, I focused on breathing, and another idea came to me. What if the future me could reach back out to me and offer me strength now? (I am a writer, and I have written all sorts of fantasy and science fiction books so go with me on this.)

I liked that idea. The future me of tomorrow, as well as the future me of a year from now, two years from now, and on and on could reach back to me and help send me strength so that I could one day join them.

I smiled at the idea as wacky as it was, but I liked it. I felt comforted in knowing that the "me" of the future could help me today.

Yes, it's a goofy idea, but it helped calm me.

Today is all we have. The present is where we can ground ourselves and find peace. If we focus too much on the past or the future, we might get lost in daydreaming. I'm all for some creative daydreaming but I also need to find solutions to face the problems that I have today.

For me, that means taking a hard look at my life. What I spend my time on, who I spend it with, and what I do.

Being healthy and balanced takes work and a clear commitment to making time to take for myself.

None of us will be at that future spot looking back at us today unless we do the work to get us there.

What choices can we make today that will help us tomorrow?

Meditation? Prayer? Exercise? Are you eating healthy? Are you sleeping enough? Are you spending time with people you love (and not just those who try to use or abuse us)?

For today, what choices will you make?

The good news is that we only need to take a few steps at a time each day. Small incremental changes over time can be the most effective ways to get us to that future.

As simple as it might sound, the phrase "one step at a time" does hold true.

DAY 91: WE ARE WHAT WE THINK

"We are what we think. All that we are arises with our thoughts. With our thoughts, we make the world." Buddha

That's a nice quote. Though scholars believe that it's not a quote from Buddha but was a rendering from Thomas Byrom, an Oxford scholar who died in 1991.

Still, no matter who wrote the words, there's a powerful message there.

In alcoholic and dysfunctional families, there is often a negative loop that runs through our heads. Self-defeating thoughts such as "we're not good enough," or "we don't deserve love and happiness."

Psychologists have coined the term **learned helplessness** to define the condition in which a person who went through a traumatic event feels that they are powerless.

If we think about the quote "we are what we think," that mindset helps us better understand who we are and how we deal with problems when they arise.

Do you feel powerless when bad things happen to you? Do you feel trapped and can't find a way out of the problem?

I believe in the importance of building a positive environment around us. I'm not saying that we should cut ourselves off from the world and stick our heads in the sand. No.

Embrace the world and see the possibilities that might not seem achievable right now.

I've gone to therapy throughout my life to help me retrain how I reactive to stress and problems. If we allow ourselves to feel trapped, then we will remain that way.

Freedom starts from within.

No one grants you freedom.

You have always had freedom if you allow yourself to be free.

People who have been in the most horrible

conditions have remained free in their hearts and mind.

What power could we unlock within if we gave ourselves that option each day?

To choose to be free from fear, abuse, anger, hate, and anxiety.

Imagine what opportunities we could embrace if we realized that we truly "are what we think."

DAY 92: SURRENDER TO JOY

There's a lot of hard work to do on ourselves. If you grew up in an alcoholic and dysfunctional family, there is a laundry list of issues that we need to work on.

But life isn't all about work.

Life isn't all about optimizing the moment to make certain that we're enhancing ourselves to be free.

No.

Sometimes we just need to laugh.

Embrace the day. Stop, look around, and take in the beauty of the world.

If you can get out into nature, go for a walk (with no phone and no music on).

Surrender to joy.

What does that mean?

Have you ever been having fun and then a rogue thought will cross through your mind: "What if something bad happens?"

It's as though we're not able to have fun without a consequence. We wait for the other shoe to drop.

What if we could put the negativity and fear out of our minds and enjoy the moment?

Surrender to joy.

The world is such a beautiful and varied place with billions of people and lots of places to visit. A walk down your street to a new store or visiting a friend whose daughter just had a baby or going to a museum to see an exhibition can unlock joy from within.

If you're wound up like a top, take a deep breath, go enjoy some fun, and unwind.

You're allowed to have fun.

Give yourself permission.

Surrender to joy.

DAY 93: IT'S OKAY TO FEEL...

It's okay to feel sad.

It's okay to feel angry.

It's okay to be happy.

Emotions are yours to express, feel, and process in your own time.

There have been many times in my life where I was told to "buck it up" and not express how I felt. But bottling emotions up inside only adds pressure to a situation, and over time, the cork pops up out of the bottle.

Finding a healthy and constructive way to express emotions is a lifelong journey. Some families repress while others wear their emotions on their sleeves.

The balance between the two might be the sweet spot. I can't say for certain because I'm not you.

How do you feel right now?

Do you do a daily check-in with how you're feeling? Are there conversations that you're dreading to have because you know that they'll result in an argument or the blame game?

With alcoholic and dysfunctional behaviors swirling around in families, you never quite know what you're going to get.

And that's when the shame comes in.

We've grown up in dysfunctional families and learning to solve conflict is not easy. Maybe you had a parent blow up at you because of something else that they were dealing with in their life, but you didn't know that at the time. Or maybe it was easier for someone in your family to repress how they felt and put on a happy face.

There are many ways you may have taken on unhealthy responses to emotion. As an adult, it's our responsibility to express our emotions healthily. What we learned and experienced as a child probably won't help us now.

Or worse, we'll be replicating unhealthy family dynamics to our children.

The basics are essential: Acknowledge how you feel.

Put a name to the emotion(s). Write them down.

If you're uncertain how to best handle the emotion you're feeling, two good places to start are writing in a journal and speaking to a therapist.

When I'm in the midst of a big problem and emotions are swirling all around me, I first admit to myself how I'm feeling. Either I write the thoughts down or have an inner monologue with myself.

Then I run through and ask:

Is it true?

(Is it true that I'm feeling sad because of X? Or, am I taking my anger out on a friend when I'm really upset because of something that happened at work?)

I like to map my emotions to what's going on in my life. I like to put my emotions in the right lane.

There's no point in taking anger out on someone else who did nothing to me.

And the same thing with trying to make someone feel guilty because I screwed up.

Emotions can be difficult to process and hard

to let go. Grief could last months. But anger could come and go in hours.

The key is feeling yourself out and taking steps to express the emotion.

Step 1: Figure out what you're feeling and why.

DAY 94: OUR GREATEST FEAR

Sure, we have lots of fears, but I wanted to be vulnerable with you for a moment and share mine with you.

I'm afraid that I'll fail my friends, family, coworkers, and yes that I'll fail you.

What do I mean by that?

I don't have all the answers, and I make mistakes like everyone else. I started this book to talk about my feelings and thoughts on growing up in an alcoholic and dysfunctional family because I wanted to shine a light on the shame and fear I've experienced in my lifetime.

I want to show people that I have felt weak, broken, and sometimes unloved.

I also wanted to talk about the challenges of overcoming destructive family patterns and how that's affected me.

So why is my fear of "not measuring up" my greatest fear?

It's complicated, and I bet a lot of you will identify with me.

As I live my life, I have worked hard to build good habits and a strong network of loved ones to help ground me.

But I am human. I fall, make mistakes, and screw up.

I fear that my loved ones will point at me and say, "See how you're acting right now? It's just like how your father was."

I know that that might not make any sense to anyone who didn't grow up in an alcoholic or dysfunctional family, but for those of you who did, I bet that line is uncomfortable for you.

I swore to myself, to God, and to all I held dear, that I would never grow up to be like my father.

The truth that I've had to face though is that the behavior patterns that I grew up with have affected me, and I've needed to work hard to make certain that I am aware of those unhealthy behaviors.

If you're not sure what I'm talking about, check out the Adult Children of Alcoholics Anonymous' laundry list.

The list contains some unflattering traits:

- low self-esteem
- live life with a viewpoint of a victim
- we try to rescue people we see as damaged
- we are terrified of abandonment

And the list goes on and on. That's frightening to me. To see myself in some of those traits and know that I was affected by behaviors outside of my control as a kid. Things that happened decades ago have influenced my initial reactions to how I handle problems.

Why would I want to admit this to the world?

Because here's the thing: I know that I'm not alone in feeling this way. And I also will not let the traits of an adult child of an alcoholic define me.

I'm choosing to shine a light of who I am because I believe that not only will it help me grow as a person, but I can help show others who feel this way that they're not alone.

There is hope.

There is a path forward.

We are not damaged goods who are undeserving of love.

We are unique and complex people with a great capacity to love and to contribute to the world.

Yes, sometimes it feels like we're going through cognitive dissonance by holding two conflicting ideas in our mind at the same time.

But here's the thing: We each have a choice. We can choose to live life as a victim and feel bad about ourselves, or we can rise up and choose to learn and practice healthy behaviors to overcome the dysfunctional behavioral traits we learned as children.

Every day we have a choice.

What will you choose?

DAY 95: STOP LIVING A LIFE OF QUIET DESPERATION

Henry David Thoreau wrote in *Walden,* "the mass of men lead lives of quiet desperation."

Do you?

Do you struggle in your life with work, family life, and try to get by?

I see so many people looking to numb themselves with alcohol, drugs, sex, or anything to get them through the pain that they are living.

Even the rich and the famous, who we think have it so easy, struggle no matter the amount of money they have.

The choice is whether we will continue to live in desperation or if we will live to our full potential.

Do you want to continue to suffer and get by?

Or, perhaps, is there another way?

What if you took ownership of your life and saw new possibilities on how to live?

Not living like a victim but embracing life and making choices that are healthy and grounding for you?

The choices that we make today will allow us to grow into who we are tomorrow.

If we want to live to our full potential, no one is going to come and save us. We must find the road ourselves. That might mean stumbling, falling, getting lost, and being afraid. But then we can get back up and find our way.

We have thousands of choices each day to continue to live repressed, desperate, or out of control, but we can stop that. Maybe we have numbed ourselves from the world so that we don't feel anything. We've inoculated ourselves from others so that we won't be hurt again.

To live a full life and to embrace our potential is scary as hell.

There's no singular path, and what your full potential is will probably be different than another.

But imagine waking up and feeling free. Or

imagine being on the path or using our physical, emotional, and spiritual muscles to keep us strong.

We don't wake up and go: "Today, I will now be whole, and all my concerns and worries will melt away" (as you flourish a wave of your magic wand).

Life isn't like that.

The journey stretches out beyond today and we cannot know where it ends. We only have today in front of us.

The habits, choices, and love we give today will help pave tomorrow's road.

How to stop living a life of quiet desperation?

Take a chance on yourself and grow.

Sign up for a new class, take out the paints and brushes again, find that job you always wanted, thaw your heart and be willing to love, embrace yourself with love like you fully deserve.

Desperation is a trap within our minds.

When you clear away the illusion, then you can be free.

DAY 96: YOU'RE EXACTLY WHERE YOU NEED TO BE

This might sound counter-intuitive, and you might get angry that you're not farther along on your self-healing journey.

I get it.

I've been there.

When I was younger, I always wanted to get to the finish line. To succeed and know that I did the job and got it done.

But life isn't really like that.

There are mile markers along the journey of life, but the only true finish line is when we die.

Every day we have is a gift.

We might want to speed up time or slow it

down sometimes, but we're at the point in the journey where we're at.

The choice is whether we're going to continue to move forward on our journey or fight against self-growth and change.

If you're reading this, then I expect that you've decided to be open-minded to self-reflection and growing as an individual.

That's great.

In life, we go through good and bad times. The part that we're in right now might be hard to deal with and be outside of our control (sickness or dealing with the loss of a loved one). We might want to fast-forward through those times, but we can't.

What we can do is accept our current situation and focus on taking care of ourselves.

If we could sum up all of our experiences and see them in a flipbook, we could better understand what challenges helped to prepare us for what we'll be doing in the future. But we can't see what will happen tomorrow.

So, we're here today. Right now.

Instead of trying to rush to the finish line, I'm learning to be happy with the present. Yes, even if that present is filled with hardship. I'm not saying that I like hardship, but acceptance is a good thing to learn.

Knowing what we can change and what we can't, can help us deal with who we want to be.

If we're dealing with hardship, what can we do today to overcome it?

And if the challenge is beyond our control (i.e., sickness), how will we respond to it?

In the end, we have ourselves. Are we good to ourselves?

Do we truly see the beauty and power each of us has?

And most importantly, do we love ourselves? Not in an egocentric way but unconditionally.

That's the thought to take in mind today.

You are exactly where you need to be.

If you're going through hardship, then what can you do to overcome that?

DAY 97: FINDING CALMNESS

Chaos, disruption, and turmoil might be all around us.

But when we are at peace, that's when we know the best course of action.

If we're stressed, running, can't stop to think, that's often when we react rather than taking time to make a decision that is helpful and healing.

Go, go, go—that's the motto of the modern world. We're supposed to juggle the job, family life, and always be connected with our mobile phone.

Why?

Because that's what "they" say.

I remember back before the time of mobile

phones and how I seemed to get along fine back then. I didn't need to take a picture of my breakfast to show the world what a great stack of pancakes I had to eat.

The challenge with modern life is putting up (and maintaining) a boundary to allow yourself time to relax and rest.

How can we be calm if we're sleeping at night, and our phone is buzzing from all the notifications?

There are Facebook posts to like, Instagram feeds to see, TikToks to make, and people to get back to on WhatsApp or Twitch.

When we put down the stress and walk away from it, we give our minds and hearts time to feel and to breathe.

Sit still in a quiet room and just breathe deeply for five minutes. The five minutes you spend relaxing will do you a world of good.

Find calmness and peace of mind instead of the never-ending scroll on our phones.

You'll feel better and might discover you like it.

DAY 98: THE POWER OF TRUSTING YOURSELF

Trust can be hard at times. Trust in family members who let us know when we needed them most, trust in what's "right and fair" in the world, but there's also an important step of trusting yourself.

Self-trust can be a no brainer for many of us. How could we not trust ourselves?

But that's not necessarily true for those of us who grew up in alcoholic and dysfunctional families.

Pity might be construed to be love. Or worse, wanting to "rescue" someone so that you can show your love to someone.

Decisions about trust happen every day and we don't often think about it.

Do we trust the airline pilot? Or the bus driver? Or the company that we work for to pay us?

But there are decisions that could be looped into shame, guilt, and fear that cause us to doubt ourselves.

If you're not sure whether the decision you are making is a healthy one (a decision that you can trust), I find asking this question helpful:

Is it healthy for me?

But more importantly, each of us needs to develop our adult voice. We typically have several voices within us:

Parent: "Don't have that piece of candy before dinner."

Child: "I want the candy now!"

Adult: "Is it healthy for me to have the candy now?"

Developing and enriching our adult voice takes practice, time, and sometimes is filled with trial and error.

We might make a decision based off of how we grew up. For example, if we try to get our kid to eat broccoli but conveniently seem to forget how we hated eating it as a kid.

A healthy balance between what's healthy,

our boundaries, and the fine line between the two, can be difficult to navigate.

If you're tired, angry, thirsty or hungry, take care of your body first. Before making a big decision, give yourself the time you need to process the decision. Reactionary decisions often do more harm than good.

Asking for some space (a reasonable amount of time and not trying to stall or be indecisive), is perfectly within your right.

When you work on building your own space to be an adult, you're carving space as a boundary to mark where you stand, who you are, and why you will say "no" to certain decisions.

Is this easy?

For an adult child of an alcoholic/dysfunctional family, no, it's not.

Guilt, fear, shame, and anger might cloud your mind and make it harder for you to trust.

Trust takes time to build.

Not only with another but with yourself.

DAY 99: CROSSING THE FINISH LINE

When presented with a glass of water and asked, "Is the glass half full or half empty?" I always reply, "half full." But a few years back, one of my friend's kids came to me and told me that the glass is always full.

Since there are molecules in the air (Oxygen, Hydrogen, Carbon Dioxide, etc.), the glass is never empty.

I laughed because it was true.

I took something that I thought I knew and saw, made a judgment, and stuck to that. But when looked at in another way, a glass is always full because we don't live in a vacuum.

In life, we like to add artificial passages of time

and goals to our lives. We celebrate when we turn 18, 21, have our 20th anniversary and a whole list of other dates.

But on a personal level, what does it mean to be "near the finish line"?

When we are in a race, we can see the line that we need to cross. As a runner, I've had to push through and cross that finish line time after time. But what does "crossing the finish line" really mean?

We're never truly really "done" with anything. If we are working on achieving a goal and want to cross the finish line, we can choose to dissociate ourselves with the event, and move on, but the memory of that time will stay with us.

I wonder what life would be like if we focus on each day and flip the meaning of "ending the race."

In life, we have a string of days that stretch out to a time that is unknown to us. If we're running a race, sure, we can cross the finish line, but we often have other races in life or want to continue training to keep our bodies in shape.

An arbitrary deadline or goal might be helpful in the short term, but I like to look at the larger picture.

Just because I graduated college doesn't mean I'm done with learning.

When I finished my first novel 30 years ago, I can still have those characters be in other stories.

Even if loved ones have passed on, their memory lives on in us.

Time is illusionary and yet so constant for us.

If we think that we're ending one part of our lives, I suggest thinking about opening yourself up to new and exciting possibilities.

We might cross the finish line, but we're still on the journey in life.

If you are newly retired, how else can you be of service to others?

New to marriage, what fun can you explore in building a relationship with your partner?

And how can you also strengthen your connections with your friends and family apart from your spouse?

When you cross the finish line of one part of your life, what other ways can you explore, grow, and give?

DAY 100: A NEW BEGINNING

We're at day 100, and I look back at the other 99 days and feel a sense of peace. We've explored a lot together over that time, and the most important message that I've discovered is that each of us matters.

We have something wonderful to share with the world.

The good that we all can do starts from within.

External validation is not our driving force. What matters is that we believe and love ourselves.

Let's think about that for a bit. If we chase after other people's validations, we'll be constantly led by feelings of insecurity. What our boss thinks about us doesn't matter in the long run. Neither does what our spouse thinks of us.

That might sound controversial at first, but is it truly?

Yes, we can receive feedback from those all around us, but our driving motivation and our self-worth are driven from within.

We do not need someone else to love us in order to love ourselves.

As adult children of alcoholics and dysfunctional families, often, fear of abandonment is strong in us. When we needed a stable person in our lives as kids, we often didn't get that.

Now that we're adults turning to another or an addiction to fuel our self-worth would be perpetuating a cycle of generational dysfunction.

The new beginning that we've embarked on is seeing that we matter.

If you can look yourself in the mirror, smile, and say, "I love myself," that is a strong first start.

The skills we need to practice in our lives are laid out in this book, and in many others like it.

We need to take care of our body, mind, and spirit and focus on our boundaries.

The new beginning that's before us is a path

of self-exploration and the freedom to live a life of happiness.

You deserve to be happy. Not because I say so, but that you are intrinsically worthy.

The challenge is: What are you going to do about it?

Making lasting good habits is hard but not impossible.

I hope you make time each day to take care of yourself and to build upon the habits we've explored in this book. I invite you to go back, read the pages again (by picking a random entry each day), and to allow yourself to be loved.

If you believe yourself worthy and open yourself up to the world, possibilities will become available to you in ways that you could not have foreseen.

If not today, then when?

ALSO BY RON VITALE

Non-Fiction Books by Ron Vitale

Thank you for reading this book. I invite you to check out the other books I have written.

Let Go and Be Free

- *Let Go and Be Free: 100 Daily Reflections for Adult Children of Alcoholics (Volume 1)*
- *Let Go and Be Free: 100 New Daily Reflections for Adult Children of Alcoholics (Volume 2)*
- *Let Go and Be Free: 100 More Daily Reflections for Adult Children of Alcoholics (Volume 3)*
- *Let Go and Be Free: 100 Final Daily Reflections for Adult Children of Alcoholics (Volume 4)*

RESOURCES

Test to get your Adverse Childhood Experiences (ACE) score: https://www.npr.org/sections/health-shots/2015/03/02/387007941/take-the-ace-quiz-and-learn-what-it-does-and-doesnt-mean

Adult Children of Alcoholics Anonymous: https://adultchildren.org/

You are Awesome by Neil Pasricha: https://www.ronvitale.com/blog/2019/9/28/you-are-awesome-how-to-navigate-change-wrestle-with-failure-and-live-an-intentional-life

. . .

Cathy Heller's Don't Keep Your Day Job podcast:
   https://www.dontkeepyourdayjob.com/podcast

A Beautiful Day in the Neighborhood movie review:
   https://www.ronvitale.com/blog/2019/11/24/a-beautiful-day-in-the-neighborhood-film-review

Popular Science. This untranslatable Danish word is the key to lowering stress:
   https://www.popsci.com/danish-word-pyt-stress-relief-psychology/

Adam Grant:
   https://www.adamgrant.net/

Brené Brown The power of vulnerability:

https://www.youtube.com/watch?t=7s&v=iCvmsMzlF7o

Card Game Goop!
https://www.ronvitale.com/blog/2013/5/4/goop-play-another-card-game

Quarter of Americans don't read books
https://www.cnbc.com/2019/01/29/24-percent-of-american-adults-havent-read-a-book-in-the-past-year--heres-why-.html

Visualization and anxiety-freeing meditations
https://www.ronvitale.com/let-go-and-be-free/2019/11/25/day-2-how-to-deal-with-the-stress-and-anxiety-from-ruminative-thoughts

The Serenity Prayer
https://en.wikipedia.org/wiki/Serenity_Prayer

. . .

10 Common Personality Traits of Adult Children of Alcoholics
https://americanaddictioncenters.org/blog/10-traits-of-adult-children-of-alcoholics

Most People Fail to Achieve Their New Year's Resolution.
https://www.inc.com/marla-tabaka/why-set-yourself-up-for-failure-ditch-new-years-resolution-do-this-instead.html

Dieting does not work, UCLA researchers report
http://newsroom.ucla.edu/releases/Dieting-Does-Not-Work-UCLA-Researchers-7832

The Power of Habit: Why We Do What We Do in Life and Business
https://amzn.to/3xUi6sI

Andrea Bocelli's Time to Say Goodbye
https://www.youtube.com/watch?v=g3ENX3aHlqU

. . .

Video of a baby laughing
    https://www.youtube.com/watch?v=RP4abiHdQpc&feature=emb_logo

Carl Sagan and "We are star stuff."
    https://www.youtube.com/watch?v=tLPkpBN6bEI

Brené Brown "What Being Sober Has Meant to Me"
    https://brenebrown.com/blog/2019/05/31/what-being-sober-has-meant-to-me/

Brené Brown *The Gifts of Imperfection: Let Go of Who You Think You're Supposed to Be and Embrace Who You Are.*
    https://amzn.to/2ZXhDcN

Brené Brown. "Call to Courage"
    https://www.youtube.com/watch?v=gr-

WvA7uFDQ

Gay Henricks *Learning to Love Yourself*
	https://www.amazon.com/Learning-Love-Yourself-Hendricks-Ph-D/dp/1439274290

This untranslatable Danish word is the key to lowering stress
	https://www.popsci.com/danish-word-pyt-stress-relief-psychology/

Magic Maze
	https://www.amazon.com/Dude-Games-Magic-Maze-Board/dp/B06XDVNNYX

Forbidden Island
	https://www.amazon.com/Gamewright-317-Forbidden-Island-Card/dp/B003D7F4YY

Better Without Booze
	https://www.

betterwithoutbooze.com/beverages

Hibiscus Fizz non-alcoholic drink
https://www.betterwithoutbooze.com/beverages/2017/7/15/hibiscus-fizz

Ron Vitale "The Mission"
https://www.ronvitale.com/blog/2016/1/30/the-mission-my-first-short-story

Ron Vitale *Dorothea's Song*
https://www.ronvitale.com/the-realms-fantasy-series

Ron Vitale *Cinderella's Secret Witch Diaries*
https://www.ronvitale.com/lost-cinderellas-secret-witch-diaries-book-1

Harmeet Kaur. "When does the decade begin and end anyway?"

https://www.cnn.com/2019/12/21/us/when-does-the-decade-end-begin-trnd/index.html

Yoga with Adriene YouTube channel
   https://www.youtube.com/user/yogawithadriene

"The Healing Self" YouTube video by Deepak Chopra
   https://www.youtube.com/watch?v=7r0NtiveG2Y

Harriet Lerner. "The Dance of Anger: A Woman's Guide to Changing the Patterns of Intimate Relationships."
   https://www.amazon.com/Dance-Anger-Changing-Patterns-Relationships/dp/0062319043

Thirty-one card game
   https://en.wikipedia.org/wiki/Thirty-one_(card_game)

. . .

Parcheesi Board Game
   https://amzn.to/3DkK4z2

Longwood Gardens
   https://longwoodgardens.org/

Louisa May Alcott *Little Women*
   https://amzn.to/3o0wEO5

Paulo Coelho *Warrior of the Light: A Manual*
   https://www.amazon.com/Warrior-Light-Manual-Paulo-Coelho/dp/0060527986

Paulo Coelho *The Alchemist*
   https://www.amazon.com/Alchemist-Paulo-Coelho/dp/0062315005

Deepak Chopra's and Oprah's 21-Day Meditation Experience
   https://chopracentermeditation.com/experience

. . .

Laundry list from Adult Children of Alcoholics
https://adultchildren.org/literature/laundry-list/

Fists of anger yoga practice
https://www.youtube.com/watch?v=wK0F2ktHsBE

Yoga with Adriene on YouTube: Dealing with anger
https://www.youtube.com/watch?v=ie5yjNGLxfQ

The Mediterranean Diet
https://www.mayoclinic.org/healthy-lifestyle/nutrition-and-healthy-eating/in-depth/mediterranean-diet/art-20047801

Brené Brown's TED Talk: Listening to Shame
https://www.youtube.com/watch?

v=psN1DORYYV0

Guido Henkel *Zen of eBook Formatting: A Step-by-step Guide to Format ebooks for Kindle and EPUB*
    https://www.amazon.com/Zen-eBook-Formatting-Step-step-ebook/dp/B00KJAH4HS

Atman
    https://www.britannica.com/topic/atman

Malala becomes youngest person ever to win the Nobel Prize
    http://www.bbc.co.uk/newsbeat/article/29566255/malala-becomes-youngest-person-ever-to-win-nobel-prize

Ending scene to Terrence Malick's film To the Wonder
    https://youtu.be/bl9s_AWUU6s?t=85

. . .

The Band's Visit
  https://en.wikipedia.org/wiki/The_Band%27s_Visit_(musical)

Answer Me song from The Band's Visit
  https://www.youtube.com/watch?v=z5jJCBQKATg

Adult Children of Alcoholics' laundry list
  https://adultchildren.org/literature/laundry-list/

Free author tools
  https://www.ronvitale.com/blog/2016/4/9/5-powerful-author-tools-for-indie-writers

Amanda Palmer's TED Talk "The Art of Asking"
  https://youtu.be/xMj_P_6H69g

Adam Grant *Originals: How Non-Conformists Move the World*

https://amzn.to/3Ev3Ucq

Charles Duhigg *The Power of Habit: Why We Do What We Do in Life and Business* https://amzn.to/3xUi6sI

Graham Kates "Doctors call for investigation after 3 migrant children in custody die of flu" https://www.cbsnews.com/news/doctors-call-for-investigation-after-3-migrant-children-in-custody-die-of-flu/

What's Your Myers-Briggs Personality Type https://en.wikipedia.org/wiki/Myers%E2%80%93Briggs_Type_Indicator#/media/File:MyersBriggsTypes.png

Carl Sagan "Pale blue dot." https://www.goodreads.com/quotes/230027-look-again-at-that-dot-that-s-here-that-s-home-that-s

. . .

Loving-Kindness meditation
    https://www.ronvitale.com/let-go-and-be-free/2019/12/7/day-15-practicing-the-loving-kindness-meditation

Let Go and Be Free private Facebook group
    https://facebook.com/groups/letgoandbe

Amanda Palmer and the Art of Asking Philadelphia 2014 Tour Stop
    https://www.ronvitale.com/blog/2014/11/15/amanda-palmer-and-the-art-of-asking-philadelphia-2014-tour-stop

Qing Li "'Forest Bath' Is Great for Your Health. Here's How to Do It"
    https://time.com/5259602/japanese-forest-bathing/

Dave Kerpen *The Art of People*
    https://www.amazon.com/Art-People-Simple-Skills-Everything/dp/0241250781

. . .

Cognitive dissonance https://en.wikiquote.org/wiki/Cognitive_dissonance

ABOUT THE AUTHOR

Ron Vitale is a fantasy and science fiction author. Influenced by the likes of Tolkien, Margaret Atwood, C. S. Lewis, and Philip Pullman, he has a Master's degree in English Literature from Villanova University where he studied the works of Alice Walker and Margaret Atwood. For his thesis, he interpreted Walker's and Atwood's novels through a psychological Jungian approach by showing how the central female protagonists use storytelling as a means to heal themselves from trauma. He lives in a small town outside of Philadelphia, Pennsylvania, and keeps himself busy by writing his blog and on learning how to be a good father to his kids all while working on his next book.

Learn more about all of the books written by Ron Vitale at www.ronvitale.com

www.ingramcontent.com/pod-product-compliance
Lightning Source LLC
Chambersburg PA
CBHW072141100526
44589CB00015B/2037